THE WHICH? GUIDE TO COMPUTERS

About the author

Since working for a decade in the software industry Richard Wentk has been a freelance writer, computer trainer and consultant, with a particular interest in making computer technology accessible to non-technical people.

THE WHICH? GUIDE
TO COMPUTERS

RICHARD WENTK

CONSUMERS' ASSOCIATION

Which? Books are commissioned and researched by
Consumers' Association and published by
Which? Ltd, 2 Marylebone Road, London NW1 4DF

Distributed by The Penguin Group:
Penguin Books Ltd, 27 Wrights Lane, London W8 5TZ

First published September 1995
Reprinted January, March 1996
Revised edition September 1996
Reprinted September, October 1997
Copyright © 1995, 1996 Which? Ltd

British Library Cataloguing in Publication Data
Wentk, Richard
   Which? Guide to Computers – (Which?
   Consumer Guides)
   I. Title II. Series
   004

ISBN 0 85202 629 3

With thanks to Sara Edlington, John Docherty, Fionna Johnson,
Ian Kilminster, Bruce Tober, Ivor Garfinkle, Marie Lorimer, Carol Johnson
Cover design by Ridgeway Associates
Cover photograph by Tony Stone Images/George Kamper
Illustration on pp 6–7 Kevin Jones Associates as used in *PC Guide* (Future
Publishing) Issue 1, July 1995
Typographic design by Paul Saunders

For a full list of Which? books, please write to Which? Books,
Castlemead, Gascoyne Way, Hertford X, SG14 1LH

Typeset by Litho Link Ltd, Welshpool, Powys, Wales
Printed and bound by Firmin-Didot (France), Group Herissey,
No d'impression: **40522**.

CONTENTS

Anatomy of a personal computer

Keyboard
The keyboard and the mouse are still the main way of telling your computer what you want it to do. The keyboard is very much like the standard typewriter keyboard with an extra set of keys for numbers on the right-hand side and various other special keys which are used by some software.

Screen/Monitor
The screen is where information is displayed, and you can see what your computer is doing. Screens vary in size, but even the smallest are capable of displaying photographs clearly.

Speakers
Many computers now come with speakers which are used for playing music and adding sound effects to software. These have serious uses beyond entertainment. For example, voice recordings can be added to computer documents, and video clips can have sound included.

Mouse
The mouse sits under your hand with the connecting lead at the top under your fingertips. As you move it around, a pointer on the screen follows your motions. You select on-screen options with the mouse buttons, which are also under your fingertips.

Joystick
This optional extra is used solely for games.

Base unit
This is the part of the computer that does all the work. All the extras
plug into the base unit. Base units come in different shapes and sizes.
Some stand upright on the desk, and some are designed to stand on
the floor. All modern computers include a fan to keep the insides cool.

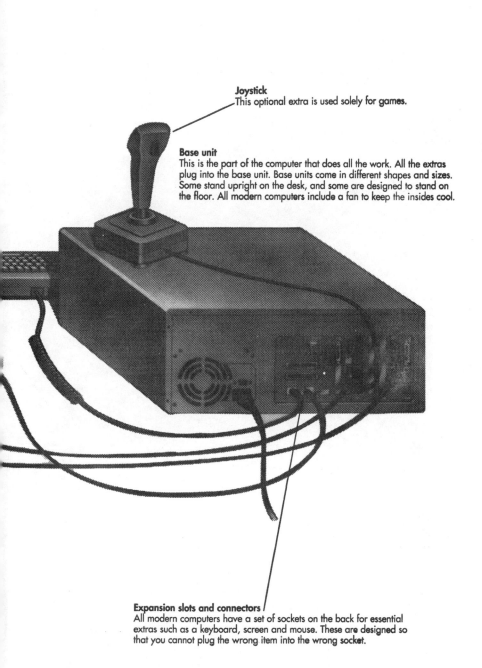

Expansion slots and connectors
All modern computers have a set of sockets on the back for essential
extras such as a keyboard, screen and mouse. These are designed so
that you cannot plug the wrong item into the wrong socket.

INTRODUCTION

AT THE beginning of the 1990s the selling of computers began to shift from specialist high-technology outlets into the high street. Today consumer spending on computer products rivals that of many established high-street goods and services. Software sales in Europe during the last three months of 1995 totalled over £1.5 billion, and interest in electronic information services such as the Internet has been raised to fever pitch by the computer press. Price wars have sent the cost of components spiralling downwards and made it possible for almost anyone to afford technology that in the mid-1980s would have been beyond the reach of all but the largest organisations. A typical mid-price computer today is far more powerful than a £1 million machine of the mid-1980s.

But for all the technological advances, the biggest obstacle facing anyone thinking of buying a computer is still the dearth of simple, easy-to-understand information. Surprisingly, perhaps, this is not just a question of jargon but also of approach. Although computers are now very much a part of everyday life, both at home and in the office, and manufacturers are making efforts to ensure that their products are easier to use, far too much useful information is still presented in the form of technical specifications. To most people such details are irrelevant. They want to know whether the computer can help them achieve what they want to achieve in their work; how much a system is likely to cost; and where they can get help if they run into problems.

A 1996 survey of over 25,000 UK companies by information technology analysts Banner (BCRS) found that fewer than one in four self-employed people uses a computer. The proportion rises to one in three for companies with five staff or less. Even among medium-sized companies with fewer than 50 staff, four out of ten had yet to computerise.

These statistics could be said to indicate a widespread reluctance to take advantage of computer technology. If companies find buying a computer this daunting, it is hardly surprising that individual consumers, who are much less likely to have access to professional support, consider buying a computer system something of a challenge. Computers are still sometimes seen as inaccessible, specialist tools, and potentially a waste of time and money for those not technically-minded enough to use them properly. Certainly there are risks involved in buying and using a computer, and a number of businesses have come to grief over ill-advised attempts to invest in computer technology. These risks can be minimised, however, and for those willing to ignore the hype and base their choice of computer on a realistic assessment of their needs the benefits can be enormous. Most companies which take the plunge and computerise some areas of their operation discover they are able to streamline and simplify much of the day-to-day maintenance of their business and make significant savings.

This book has been written for the non-technical person who would like to know more about buying a computer as a practical office tool, rather than as a grey box with an attached set of performance statistics. In the pages that follow you will find simple explanations of what a computer can do for your business, how to choose between competing products, how to estimate the real costs of a computer system, and how to make sure that you and your business are protected if things go wrong. Also included are suggestions to help you guard against the common pitfalls of computer purchase, together with hints and tips on how to save money by negotiating better prices and buying wisely. Many of the common jargon words are explained, to enable you to read and understand advertisements and articles in computer magazines. Other areas covered include the pros and cons of the Internet and other electronic information services, the legal implications of maintaining a computer system, information on how to finance your purchase, how a computer affects your tax position, and how to ensure that continuous use of computer equipment and accessories will not damage your health.

If you are to get the best from your investment, your computer system has to be matched to your individual requirements. The information presented here will help you clarify what you want, and give you the tools and confidence to deal with computer traders competently. Whether you are running a medium-sized business or simply looking for a better way to write letters and do your personal accounts, you will find everything you need in this book to help you acquire a useful and productive tool for your work.

CHAPTER 1

WHAT A COMPUTER CAN DO FOR YOU

A COMPUTER is the perfect tool for manipulating information. In the office it can replace the ageing typewriter, act as a very fast adding machine and provide easy access to the books and other records. In the home it can be used for writing letters, entertaining and educating children, playing games and managing personal finances.

However, any modern machine, even a modest one, can be used for much more than these tasks. In fact, a computer can be used to help with almost anything, from automating a bakery to keeping track of stock in a bookshop or displaying examples of different hairstyles to customers with their own features superimposed electronically.

The term 'information' is very wide; it covers words, sounds, photographs and numbers. Even images such as maps and technical drawings can be stored and manipulated on most modern computers. New uses, such as photographic editing and retouching, interior design and automated route planning are beginning to appear in sophisticated forms.

A computer is a sizeable investment. Used wisely, it can streamline the running of any business. Unfortunately, it can also become more of a problem than a solution. It is possible to cripple a business by making the wrong decision in purchasing and using a computer system. Using real-life examples this book illustrates the sorts of mistakes people make regularly and how you can avoid them.

CASE HISTORY: Jenny

Jenny Shipway, who runs a clothing business, was looking for a computer to help with business administration.

'A friend suggested I got a computer to help with the books. This sounded like a great idea, so we started to look around at what was available and eventually decided on a PC.

'So I got the computer first. Now I know that was my first mistake. I should have got the software sorted out and then found the right computer for it. I had an idea that somehow the computer on its own would make everything easier. I hadn't even thought about software for it at all. There was some free stuff that came with it, but it didn't seem to do much. It certainly wasn't what I wanted.

'On my friend's suggestion I had a look round some of the computer shops in Tottenham Court Road, London. In a lot of them the sales people leapt on you the second you walked through the door. I felt pretty intimidated.

'Eventually I found one shop that was slightly more relaxed. I explained that I was running a business and needed some software for it. I was steered in the direction of a software package described as an "office suite". I asked if it would do what I wanted and was told that it was perfect for businesses. Exactly what I was looking for. It cost nearly £450. That sounded a lot, but I thought that if it did the job it would be worth it.

'It didn't do the job, and it wasn't worth it. I found it was much too complicated. I eventually got the word processor and the electronic organiser working, but the rest of it was beyond me. It wasn't what I wanted at all. I'm sure if I was running a big company it would be just the thing, but for my kind of small business, doing the sales, bought ledger and VAT, it just wasn't right.

'In desperation I bought a few computer magazines. I didn't understand much of the editorial content, but I saw what I'd just bought being advertised for £250! That was the going rate, because of something called a "competitive upgrade". I'd paid the full recommended retail price, when I could have saved myself nearly half of that. Never mind that it didn't do what I wanted anyway.

'Of course I was furious, but there was nothing I could do. I realise it was my own fault, as I wasn't clear about what I needed and I didn't *think things through. Computers have this aura of infallibility, and it's easy to feel intimidated and make decisions you'd never dream of in another context.*

'I tried contacting the shop but of course they said they couldn't take the software back. I'd broken the seal and started using it, and that, as far as they were concerned, was that. I even contacted my lawyer, but he said that in the circumstances I'd be pushing my luck trying to take action.

'I think that was the worst moment. At that point I'd spent the best part of £2,000 and had nothing to show for it, apart from some letters printed out more stylishly than I could have achieved on a typewriter and a slightly better organised address book. Someone suggested I tried ringing around computer consultants listed in Yellow Pages. *A few were off-hand and said that they only dealt with larger companies. One or two simply didn't return my calls. But eventually I got through to someone who very patiently listened to what I wanted, gave me some options, and we settled for a proper accounts system. It cost all of £100, and it does everything – accounts, tax, VAT, PAYE, the lot. He even helped me get it working, showed me how to use it and helped me sell the "office suite" to someone else. Apparently I hadn't registered it, so I wasn't even the official owner. We managed to get nearly £200 for it. Unfortunately, that money went on his fee. That hurt a bit, but I do think it was worth it.*

'I realise now that it's easy to waste a fortune in this game. If I was doing it all again I'd make damn sure I did my homework. Either that or that I'd real expert help from someone who's been down the same path. That's just so important – otherwise I'd have wasted the best part of £2,000, and been left with nothing to show for it at all.'

Software first

A quick look through some computer magazines shows that most advertising concentrates on hardware. Computers are sold as boxes, rather than useful tools. The industry works on the basis that hardware is exciting, doubly so if it works faster than last year's hardware. Software, which is what turns the hardware into a useful tool, appears to be something of an afterthought.

When deciding on a computer system, it is important to approach things from the other end: software, then hardware. You have tasks that need to be carried out. A computer may be able to help you with them. So take a look at the software available and decide which package you might find useful for which tasks.

Managing your money

A computer can be an invaluable tool for managing your money. At its simplest it can help you balance the books and perform cheque-book reconciliations. With the help of a computer you can keep a history of all your transactions which is at least as detailed as that kept by your bank. This can make domestic budgeting easier – you can, for example, keep a detailed record of heating and lighting bills on a quarterly basis, and be ready for the next set of bills well before they arrive. Another possible use is to check annual percentage rate and mortgage calculations, so that you can work out exactly how expensive a loan will be and find the most cost-effective way to pay it off.

CASE HISTORY: Steven

Steven Adams works from home as a freelance journalist. Before he got a computer, he had problems keeping on top of his financial situation.

'I'm not a very organised person. I love working from home, and also having the opportunity to get out there and chase stories rather than being stuck in an office. But I always used to get my accounts in late, and I'd usually be charged interest by the Inland Revenue. I was hopeless at keeping track of invoices, too. Sometimes I wouldn't even bother sending them in. But it's a bad habit to get into, as you have no idea where your money is coming from or who owes you what. It was getting so bad that my accountant took me to one side at one point and politely suggested that I needed to get my act together.

'Even though it should only take maybe a half-hour a week to sort out all my expenses, somehow I just couldn't seem to find the time. So I started to wonder if my computer could help. I knew that all I needed was some software.

'The first thing I tried was a spreadsheet. This wasn't what I wanted at all. For a financial whizz it would be perfect, but for me it was just

too involved. It was too open-ended and I didn't fancy having to program it myself before I could start using it.

'So I had a good, long think about what I needed. I decided it had to be something that was designed from the start to do the things I wanted. It should be able to track my invoices and then remind me when payments were late. I also needed help keeping track of the expenses that come up on each job. If I don't note these down I end up paying tax on the money that's refunded to me. Then I needed some general accounting and bookkeeping help, and also something that could work out expenses incurred as part of my job in a more general way, like petrol, phone bills and so on. Finally I needed something that was easy to set up and use. I'm not VAT-registered, so that wasn't a problem. But a VAT option would be useful.

'The next step was to go into a newsagent and buy a pile of computer magazines. Most of the adverts were hardware-based. But there were a few software products listed too.

'Eventually I tried a demonstration copy of some bookkeeping software that came free with a magazine. It was a limited version, but I tried it out and found that it did almost everything the way I wanted it done. The full version was only £100, so I got that, and got organised. I bought the version with the VAT option and now that work is picking up I don't have to worry about hiring an accountant every so often to sort things out. It's great, because the software paid for itself right away.'

Bookkeeping

For most businesses keeping the books is something of a chore. A computer can automate the work, as well as producing professional end-of-year accounts. Keeping up with VAT calculations can also be made much less time-consuming. It is relatively simple to automate VAT accounting including any rate changes and zero-rated items. It is also possible to produce a single printout at the end of the accounting period which can be sent straight to HM Customs and Excise with a covering letter.

CASE HISTORY: Stella

Stella Beck runs a stationery supply company.

'Bookkeeping has never interested me, but it's never seemed cost-effective to employ someone to do it. I used to be very disorganised about it, and sometimes I'd lose bills and forget to chase payments.

'I bought a simple accounts and money management package, and it has really helped. I'm disciplined enough now to make sure that all the sales and payments go through the system, and at the end of the day it tells me exactly where I stand. It's been a godsend for the VAT, because that used to take forever. Now, I just have a printout I can wave at the Customs and Excise people. They're happy because they don't need to hassle me, I'm happy because it takes an hour to sort everything out instead of a couple of days of panic. The business is happier too. I have more time to deal with people, which is the part I really enjoy.'

Sole traders can use a computer to keep track of their creditors and debtors. This can be combined with invoice- and cheque-printing systems, to provide an all-in-one cash flow control system. It is possible to set up a system whereby bad debts are chased with letters, as well as making sure that bills are paid as late as possible to help with cash flow. One advantage of a system like this is that it enables you to estimate accurately the financial position of your business a month or two ahead, based on sales projections.

Advanced accounting systems can handle credits and debits in foreign currencies, and allow for exchange-rate fluctuations. The job of calculating payroll contributions is also relatively straightforward. The computer can be made to allow for budget and tax changes and even refer to them on a year-by-year basis. Keeping track of payroll outgoings, PAYE and National Insurance contributions becomes much simpler.

Financial planning

For financial planning the spreadsheet is now an indispensable tool of the trade. It presents you with a grid of boxes, called 'cells', each of which contains either a number or a formula. You can specify something as simple as 'add up all the numbers entered above and print the total here', or as complex as the total payment for a loan, based on a principal, a period and an interest rate.

CASE HISTORY: Martin

Martin Smith, a chartered accountant, was wary of computers until one of his clients showed him a spreadsheet in action.

'I was hooked. It was just the perfect tool for the job. Most people who use spreadsheets don't have a financial background, so they only use simple applications like profit and loss accounts. I found I could do much more than that, because it's easy to do things like profit management, payback analysis and answer other 'what-if?' questions.

'Most of my work used to be tax-based, Now I get a fair bit of work helping with business plans. With the spreadsheet I can track interest rates, and watch what effect they'll have on a new project. New businesses can be very sensitive to these, so I can warn clients just how much of a risk they're taking. The fact that I can draw graphs helps as well – they can put a message over in a very direct, accessible form.'

As Martin's story shows, spreadsheets are ideal for speculative calculations. It is easy to set up a table of potential income against interest payments and then vary the interest rate to see what happens. Without a computer you would have to recalculate each entry. With a computer you can change a single number – in this case the interest rate – and the spreadsheet does the rest. The information can be presented graphically as well as in tabular form. This is useful for trend-spotting and can also help with producing financial reports for directors and shareholders.

Money on-line

Most banks now offer schemes whereby statements can be sent direct from the bank's computer to the business's computer without having to be printed on paper first. These schemes also offer the chance to make payments electronically. Money can be transferred from one account to another – which may be abroad – by typing a few commands on the computer's keyboard. These payments can be arranged at any time of the day or night.

A computer also makes it easier to keep track of stocks and shares. There are now a number of electronic news services which offer more or less up-to-the-minute details of stock prices. Combined with trend analysis software these can give you your own personal electronic connection to the Stock Exchange with 'buy' or 'sell' suggestions.

Stock control

For applications which require a more in-depth approach to information management, the best available tool is the database. A database can be used to keep track of any kind of information and pick out trends and details from it. For example, when managing a sales team it is possible to collate sales by area, by product, by salesman or by season.

Keeping track of hundreds of different items in a warehouse while working out the optimum use of space is something of a challenge by hand. But a database can be used to tackle the problem easily, as well as making it possible to play with 'what-if' scenarios.

CASE HISTORY: George

George Becker runs a car spares service. He uses a computer to keep track of stock levels and to manage his inventory in an intelligent way.

'I got someone in to set up a database for me. It keeps track of all the parts I sell, warns me when stocks are low and reminds me to re-order. It's not foolproof – every so often we'll get a run on some part or other out of the blue and I run out. But it's made my life a lot easier.

'The reports are great. I can keep track of exactly what the stock is worth and cut down on slow-selling lines so I don't have goods lying around taking up space.

'It helps with the selling too. It's all been marked up so that if one part needs an extra, that comes up on the screen. We don't get people coming back a day later saying "Can I have one of these as well?" any more.'

Another efficient use of a database is in personnel. It is easy to set up a database of employees, with photographs, to include all the details of appraisals and indications of an employee's work record. This makes it possible to arrange a 'skills bank' that can be used when employees are being selected for new projects.

Managing personal information

An electronic personal organiser can completely replace a paper one. It is a convenient way to store information such as 'to-do' lists, anniversaries, currency-conversion factors, appointment and meeting reminders and general notes. Electronic organisers can also be set up to provide an audible reminder or alarm at a certain time, and to keep links between different kinds of information. All the contact details of everyone involved on a certain project can be kept together, and appointments can be linked with telephone numbers so that any changes can be communicated quickly and easily.

CASE HISTORY: Trevor

Trevor Knight sells advertising for a magazine publishing company. He used to use a paper 'organiser' but recently switched to a computer-based system.

'I can honestly say it's changed my life. Now everything – appointments, follow-up calls, names, addresses, phone numbers, fax numbers – are all systematically stored away instead of being in an overstuffed ringbound notebook with pages and business cards spilling out of it. The computer can find anything in a fraction of a second. The fun part is getting it to dial the phone numbers and log the calls for me too.'

Communications

A computer can also be used to transmit information as well as storing it. With the addition of a simple and affordable extra called a **modem**, your computer can dial telephone numbers for you (see Appendix II). This turns a computer into an automated telephone book which can save you hours during the course of a working week.

A modem can also be used to send and receive faxes. These can be read on screen and printed out only if necessary for future reference. While many budget fax machines still use fax paper which is prone to curling, fading and yellowing, computer-printed faxes are always printed on plain paper.

CASE HISTORY: Ryan

Ryan Williams is a freelance journalist with a particular interest in learning how computers can be used to communicate.

'I bought a modem to send and receive faxes. Most of what I sent came straight from my computer anyway, so I didn't need to print it out.

'Then one of my editors told me about electronic mail. The company already used an internal mail system and was enlarging it so that outsiders could send mail as well. It meant I could send copy straight to the office without even faxing. The text would go directly from my computer to the office system. As more companies, educational establishments and individuals start to use electronic mail, the day is not far away when I will be able to send e-mail to anyone anywhere in the world.'

Within an office, computers can be connected together on a **network** so that information and messages can be passed among them. **Electronic mail (e-mail)** can take the place of paper memos, and the network can also be used to share resources such as printers and external fax machines. The biggest advantage of a network is that it makes it easy to keep track of people and make sure that everyone works together smoothly.

The **Internet** offers the same kinds of facilities but on a much larger scale. The Internet is an international computer network that allows mail to be exchanged between any computer anywhere. For example, you can mail someone on the other side of the world with a list of prices and services. Unlike ordinary mail, the information arrives almost instantaneously. Costs are based on national, and perhaps even local, call charges, no matter where the destination. Collaborative projects can also be managed and undertaken across the Internet.

The Internet can be an excellent source of computer support and advice. Aside from Internet connection charges – usually quite reasonable – this support is free and is provided by experts.

Presentation

Business presentations play an important role in many corporate environments and here too the computer can offer effective help. As with desktop publishing tools and word processors, many presentation applications offer a range of templates which can be used to add impact to a presentation. They also include libraries of graphics and symbols. The most sophisticated tools offer simple animation features which include video effects such as dissolves and cross-fades, and also animated graphs and symbols. Pre-recorded music clips and sound effects can also be used to add emphasis and interest to the presentation.

Until the 1980s all stationery was printed by professional printers. However with the advent of desktop publishing, pioneered by the Apple Computer Corporation with its Macintosh range, it is now possible for a business or an individual to produce professional-quality leaflets, flyers, posters, advertising material, business cards and so on. Desktop publishing software is available for all makes of computer, and in many cases is sold with off-the-peg design templates. These guarantee professional results and help to overcome the lack of design and layout skills which blighted many early amateur desktop publishing efforts.

CASE HISTORY: Sally

Sally Griffiths runs a computer training company.

'A big part of the job is getting information across as clearly as possible, and computers can be really good for that. Today's software makes it easy to design striking presentations, and we use those to communicate with as much impact as possible. It helps our clients to pick things up more quickly. They're also impressed when they see what a computer can do.

'We tend to work a lot with corporate teams, and they often need to use the same technology themselves. So it's a bonus that presentation software is one of the easier kinds of software to use. They can get superb results very quickly. It helps with confidence – some people are still a bit intimidated by computers – and it helps them practically too.

'We also consult on presentation and image in general, and there are some very interesting things that businesses can do with a simple black and white laser printer and pre-printed stationery'.

The automated mail-shot is another useful facility that can help with presentation. This takes a standard letter, a list of addresses and other relevant details and automatically produces a string of personalised letters (complete with printed envelopes). Targeted carefully and used creatively mail-shots can be very effective.

At the moment, most affordable computer systems print in black and white only. Over the next few years high-quality colour printers will become more widely available and affordable, but for now it is still possible to produce strikingly professional results by using pre-printed paper. These offer graphic backgrounds as an effective backdrop for text that can be added later. They can be used to produce professional-looking leaflets, letters and business cards for a much smaller outlay than something that has been designed and printed by a print-house. Another advantage is that the work can be done in-house as required to order at any time.

Professional tools for specialist work

Computers can also be used to help with specific professional applications. Job-specific software is readily available for a wide range of professions including law, medicine, architecture, design and various kinds of engineering.

CASE HISTORY: Fionna

Fionna Johnson works from home as an illustrator and graphic designer.

'Like a lot of creative people, I was very wary of computers. To be honest I thought they were rather dull. But when a friend demonstrated what he could do on his computer with graphic design software, I was smitten. Now I have similar equipment, it enables me to try out all sorts of different approaches in a fraction of the time it would take to produce alternative designs conventionally. So I can supply a far better, more flexible service to clients at a low cost.

'I now use a graphics tablet and stylus instead of a pen and paper, and "draw" into the computer directly. I can simulate any kind of brush — airbrush, watercolour, pencil, whatever — and even make the "paper" as wet or dry as I'd like. The range of colours is all but infinite. And it's easy to add extras such as fragments of photographs or news clippings, and then, if you want, distort them to produce a special effect.

'I've had a huge amount of extra work as a result, and it's really freed me up creatively. I can do things I never even dreamed of doing with ink and paper, and I still haven't reached the limits of what I can do. I don't even need to worry about mistakes. I can undo the last thing I did, and the computer takes me back to where I was before.

'The only problem is getting things printed. Detailed full-colour artwork can cost a small fortune to print out if you use a bureau, but more and more publishers now handle designs and artwork on floppy disks and data cartridges.'

Computer-aided design (CAD)

This software can be invaluable for visualising two-dimensional and three-dimensional objects. CAD software is rather like an advanced version of the traditional drawing board, except that it can be used to design in three dimensions as well as two. The drawings – which can include mechanical parts, buildings, items of furniture and so on – are held inside the computer's memory. They can then be viewed on the screen from any angle and altered quickly and easily. CAD can help with engineering, architecture, interior design and any other kind of work that can benefit from the chance to look at a plan or layout before it is drawn or built. Advanced CAD tools can be used to place computer-generated images of items on a photographic background. This is ideal for architectural work, enabling the effect of a building on its surroundings to be assessed before the building is built.

Image manipulation

More and more artists and graphic designers are using computers. Many advertising hoardings now carry work that was designed – at least in part – on a computer and computer animations are routinely used in television advertising, including spectacular '**morphing**' effects where one object appears to change into another. Computer animators such as William Latham are working with the branch of mathematics known as fractals to create intriguing new images. Computers offer designers many advantages over conventional media, including the ability to create new special effects that are not possible any other way.

Other examples

Computer technology is also influencing photography. Photographers have always used studio and darkroom techniques to enhance their work, but with a computer these kinds of adjustments or image manipulation can be made more easily using **photographic tools**.

For haulage firms and countless businesses for which getting from A to B in the fastest possible time is an important consideration, one of the most useful computer tools of recent years has been the **electronic route-planner**. This works out a route between two places based on a number of criteria (shortest, cheapest, quickest and so on). The route can be tailored to take into account typical speeds and miles-per-gallon ratings of different vehicles. Planners for roads in Europe and the United States are also available.

Another practical application is the preparation of **timetables for schools**. In the past this has been an onerous and time-consuming task, but a computer can keep track of all the information with ease.

Legal firms can now access case histories and precedents electronically. **Legal databases** are available which detail previous judgements and make it easy to track related cases. This can save many hours of research.

Even **catering and hotel management** can benefit from computerisation. Many hotels now use computers to keep track of room bookings, maintain a list of their guests' spending and calculate an itemised bill at the end of their stay.

Leisure uses

Since the late 1980s the home computer has gradually been integrated with other home entertainment and leisure products. A plug-in extra called a TV tuner is now available which transforms a computer into a television set. Many computers can now play music compact discs (CDs) through a pair of attached speakers. The same CD player can also be used to view videos, which are also supplied in CD form. Software is also being supplied on special CDs called CD-ROMs (compact disc, read-only memory). These look like ordinary music CDs but contain information instead of music. CD-ROMs have a vast storage capacity, and new kinds of **multimedia** software (which includes pictures, sounds and video clips as well as words) have been developed to take advantage of this.

Other leisure uses include art and music. With all creative applications the power of the computer is demonstrated in the ease with which beginners can correct mistakes. A musician can record a performance and then correct individual notes. The corrections can be as obvious as changing wrong notes, or as subtle as tiny changes in phrasing or rhythm. An artist can remove the last brush stroke, rub out sections of a picture without leaving any traces, or change the colours after a picture is finished. Those with slightly more dedication and enthusiasm can explore the world of computer animation and photo-realistic image creation.

There is also a small but growing market in educational software. These applications range from simple counting and reading games for pre- and primary school children, to more advanced 'adventures' in science. Some of these have obvious uses as a worthwhile and educational distraction for children whose harassed parents would like a break. A number of educational and general interest titles are aimed at adults: for example, various encyclopedias are now available in CD-ROM format. Unlike a paper encyclopedia these include snatches of sound, music and video to enhance the presentation of information.

Finally there are computer games. These are developing into an art form in their own right, and the latest games are now designed and created by the same studios that produce Hollywood films.

Choosing the right software for the job

Software comes in two types. The first is the dedicated application, specialised for a single job: for example, an accounts package, which is designed to keep the books and cannot be used for anything else. To use this kind of software you just type in your information. All the setting up has already been done for you. The second is the general-purpose package, which gives you a framework in which to work. These have to be tailored to your needs before you can use them. In this group are all the large business software packages. A spreadsheet can be used not only for accounts but for tax, financial projections, balance sheets, and mortgage and loan calculations as well. Before you attempt any of these tasks, however, you have to create a template for each one. This kind of software gives you two jobs instead of one – first you create a framework for the information, and then you add the information itself, but it has the advantage that you can organise information to suit specific needs. However, setting up the software will take extra time.

The type of software you choose will depend on the kind of work you want to do. If you want a specific job done or if you are worried about the amount of time it will take you to master a computer, then a tailor-made package is a good choice. This will give you a return much more quickly and will be easier to use and set up in the short term.

If you would like to explore what a computer can do for you in a more general way and would prefer a more flexible approach, then one of the larger business packages such as Microsoft's Office Professional may suit your needs better. Some of these are very powerful indeed, and there is often some overlap between the applications they include. For example, you could work out quarterly sales figures by geographical region using either a spreadsheet or a database. Neither is 'right' for the job. You will simply approach the problem in two different ways, depending on which you use.

If you decide on the second type you will have the added advantage of integration. Large business packages are often designed to work with each other, so you will have the ability to move information from a database to a spreadsheet, and perhaps create some charts which could then be 'pasted' into a word processor for a business report.

Is a computer essential?

Every year the computer industry spends millions of pounds in an attempt to persuade you to buy one of their products. For all this, you may find you do not need a computer at all.

CASE HISTORY: Jill

Jill Taylor runs a small newsagent's shop. She considered getting a computer to help manage the accounts and organise paper deliveries, but decided against it.

'We don't make a fortune, so we didn't have much to spend. We made a few enquiries and looked at a few computers, but in the end decided it just wasn't worth it. My husband has been doing the books for years, and he is quite happy with the way things are. He might get them done more quickly with a computer, but he says he enjoys the work. And he double-checks everything, so mistakes aren't a worry.

'As for the paper round, that takes half an hour a day to sort out. I have to write all the addresses on the papers by hand anyway, and it wouldn't be a lot quicker to use printed sticky labels. Keeping track of the payments is a bit of a chore, but I've been managing the job for a long time now and I'm used to it.

'Once we thought about it, it was obvious that we could get by without a computer. We'd have to spend over £500 to get something that was up to the job, and there seemed better things to spend the money on. In the end we just decided to leave it – and I can't honestly say I've regretted that.'

It is tempting to buy a computer 'just because'. If you look at your needs closely, however, you may decide that you do not need one at all. If you have less than £500 to spend and intend to use your computer mainly for writing letters, then it may be better to look at some of the all-in-one word processors currently available. These cost between £200 and £400, and offer you many of the features of a computer-based system. They have the advantage of being easier to use, easier to move from one place to another and easier to learn.

If you want to dabble in the basics of computing, but are not concerned about doing any serious work or keeping up with the very latest developments, then consider a second-hand machine. These are adequate for light duty work, will introduce you to all the basic concepts and can cost as little as £100. They will not be able to work with the latest software and hardware, so you should assume that you are buying a closed system. In other words, what you buy is what you get. Extras are not an option. For someone on a strict budget they can prove an excellent, low-risk introductory purchase.

If you are planning to use your computer for more business-oriented tasks, you can expect to pay £500 for a basic modern machine to over £10,000 for a no-expense-spared system. In general, you get the best compromise between cost and performance at around £1,500, for a complete system including printer and software. This will give you a modern machine that you can expand as your funds grow, but which will have a life of at least three or four years. (At the end of that period it will still be useful, but you will need to reassess your needs in light of technological advances.)

When it comes to looking at the individual facets of your business, the best approach to computerisation is to ask yourself how much time you spend on certain activities and how organised you are already. If you are perfectly happy keeping addresses and phone numbers in a card file, then you should think long and hard before buying an electronic system to replace them. In general, activities that you perform occasionally are best done by hand. Activities that are time-consuming, repetitive and a chore are best done by computer, but if you have a system that works for you now without a computer, there is no good reason why you should feel any need to buy one.

As a rough guide you can start by working out how much time you waste over the course of a year on tasks that add nothing to the value of your business. Next, calculate how much this time is worth at a suitable hourly rate. Estimate how much time these activities will take if you get a computer to help you. For some kinds of work – VAT, payroll calculations and so on – this should be relatively straightforward. You can guesstimate how long it would take to type the relevant information into the computer, and then add a week or so as 'learning time'. Other kinds of work will be much harder to quantify and you may need to arrange a demonstration at a reputable computer store before you can get an idea. Once done, you can work out the time and cost saving of installing a computer by comparing these two figures.

This is only useful as a rough guide; the installation of a computer sometimes results in improved productivity and new business opportunities which are not always foreseeable. Sometimes it doesn't. By doing this comparison, you will at least have some idea of whether you are buying on a whim or taking a calculated risk.

Now that you have an overview of what is possible, it is time to look at your options in more detail and examine more closely what you should look for when considering each one.

CHAPTER 2

BUYING A COMPUTER – AN OVERVIEW

TO GET the most from a computer you need to remember that you are not just buying a collection of gadgets and widgets, but a complete system – something that is very much greater than the sum of its parts. Computer advertising often tries to lure novice users into spending more than they need by tempting them with vague promises of speed and power. In practice, these factors can have surprisingly little to do with long-term usefulness and reliability. Buying the fastest computer in the world is a waste of time and money if you spend all your time struggling with it. Similarly, a computer that breaks down or leaves you baffled can be more of a liability than an asset.

To avoid this kind of difficulty, it is important to leave the glossy advertising to one side and look realistically at the different elements of a computer system.

Hardware describes the physical parts of the computer – keyboard, screen, main system unit and any other extras you decide to buy. Think of it as an extension to your office. Inside the computer's case you will find the equivalent of a filing cabinet for storing information and a desk-like area where you can choose from a selection of useful tools. The more you spend on hardware the more quickly these tools will do their work for you, and the more room there will be in your new 'office' for both tools and information. There are many different kinds of computer but the two most popular lines are the IBM-compatible PC (known as the PC) and the Apple Macintosh (known as the Mac).

Software describes the tools or programs which run on the hardware and more often than not you will need to buy them separately. There are hundreds, perhaps even thousands, of different kinds of software available today, all tailor-made to help you with specific kinds of work. For example, if you want to write letters or create text you need to buy word-processing software; to keep track of finances, you buy an accounting package.

Software, much more than hardware, determines how productive your computer will be. Good software is so easy to use that you forget that it is there. It is also easy to learn (**user-friendly**), which means you can start doing useful work with it very quickly. Bad software can be a hindrance, and will force you to work around it rather than work with it. It can also cause difficulties when you start to use it: for example, when your computer does something unexpected and you are left floundering and confused with no idea what to do next.

Choose your software first. This is one of the golden rules of computer-buying. Work out what you want to do, decide which software will work best, and then find the hardware to match.

The hardware and software are the most obvious parts of a computer system, but there are a number of other options you also need to consider.

Support means help with maintenance and problem-solving. If you rely on your computer on a daily basis you need to be sure that the support will be efficient and quick – being left without your computer for a week or a month can be disastrous.

The other kind of support is needed for those times when you are unable to work out what to do next. You may perhaps be using a word processor that claims you can print lettering in italics, but even though you have looked at the instruction manual you still can't see how to do this. At times like these it is a very good idea to have someone or something you can refer to – otherwise you can find yourself wasting a lot of time or using your software at a tiny fraction of its potential.

Training is closely related to support and provides you with the help you need to get started. There are numerous training resources available, some very affordable. Courses or personal tuition can prove expensive, so you may want to consider books, videos and computer-based training software. Magazines can also be a supplementary source of introductory hints and tips.

Insurance is vital to ensure that if something goes wrong, you have the financial resources to put it right. If your computer fails or is stolen you may be left without access to the information essential to the running of your business. In the short term such a loss can be crippling; in the long term it can be catastrophic. Fortunately, you can protect yourself from these kinds of risks. You can insure your system to protect the information as well as the system itself. You can also keep the information safe by making regular safety copies or backups.

Security becomes an issue when your information is confidential, or you are not the only person with access to it. There are also legal considerations to be aware of if you start to collect information about your customers or your employees (see Appendix X). There are ways to protect information and ensure that it can be read only by selected users.

The other kind of security is much simpler and cruder – you need to protect your computer against theft. This is a growing problem, especially in large towns and cities. Again, there are basic steps you can take to make sure that your equipment is as unattractive to thieves as possible. This is discussed in Chapter 10.

Space Is there sufficient or a convenient space in your existing work area? Computers, like children, can be more demanding than anyone expects. If you find that your existing office is not adequate to cope with a large new arrival, you will need to budget for extra space or furniture to cope with it.

The buying process

Once you have decided what you need and looked at the options, you can start the buying process. Don't rush into it, however. There are good ways and bad ways to buy a computer. Briefly, you are likely to have the following options:

- hire a consultant
- buy a complete package from a dealer or by mail-order
- do the research and buying yourself
- buy a second-hand system
- ask a computer-literate friend or colleague to guide you through the process.

A consultant

Hiring a consultant is by far the easiest and the least time-consuming way to buy a computer. It should also – in theory, at least – give you the best results. Unfortunately, in the short term it is by far the most expensive approach.

Consultancy fees can vary from £25 to £250 an hour; the rate depends on the consultant's experience and the size of project. Computerising a sole trader's business is relatively straightforward. Computerising a medium-sized company which has offices in different parts of the country requires a much higher level of expertise.

A good consultant should be able to:

- talk to you in detail about your requirements
- analyse your needs
- let you know if your expectations are unrealistic and discuss alternatives
- choose the best and most cost-effective solution, and settle on a firm price
- install a fully tested and working system
- provide training and advice on how to use the system most effectively, or make recommendations on the best sources for training from outside
- be on call to provide support if anything goes wrong, or arrange for professional support from another source.

One of the best ways to find a consultant is by personal recommendation. It is worth asking friends and colleagues. Do remember, however, someone who works well with a friend may not always be the right person to work with you.

If you need to start 'cold', you will find that some consultants advertise in the trade press and *Yellow Pages*. They may also run shops and small dealerships of their own. Your local dealer may know of a tried and trusted consultant.

Unfortunately, there is as yet no professional organisation which can guarantee a level of service. This means that when you are looking for a consultant you are largely on your own, and you need to apply the same skills and instincts you would use when hiring any employee.

These are some points to consider:

Professionalism You need to feel confident that your consultant will keep appointments, be professional and be on call at any reasonable time. A few consultants are technically brilliant but can be abrasive with those less knowledgeable than themselves, so unless you specifically need the services of an unusually gifted specialist avoid them.

Some parts of the computer trade can be quite informal; if the consultant turns up to your first meeting dressed casually do not assume that he or she is not professional. Don't allow first impressions to put you off – if your consultant is able it will show in the references and attitude, not necessarily in the choice of clothes.

Honesty and directness There is a small chance that you will be your consultant's first client which he or she should divulge in any initial interview. In this case it is advisable to be especially attentive to your consultant's previous work record. A good consultant will be happy to offer credentials.

It is prudent to discuss exactly what the terms of your working relationship will be and, if possible, draw up a full contract so that if there are any problems you are covered legally, and both of you know exactly where you stand.

Previous work experience A good consultant will be happy to provide details of previous clients who can offer references. Asking for these will give you an idea of the consultant's capabilities and personality – both from the answers you get to your questions and the stories previous clients have to tell.

You should also ask about the consultant's areas of expertise. A specialist may not have the skills needed to take on more general work.

Communication skills A good consultant should be able to speak plain English without intimidating you or making you feel that you are working at cross purposes. The consultant should demonstrate a clear grasp of your requirements. Be very wary of someone who tries to blind you with science or talks entirely in computer jargon.

The words 'feasibility study' should also be treated with suspicion. Putting together a computer system for a small business to handle accounts, payroll work, word processing and some desktop publishing does not require a feasibility study – although the computerising of a medium-sized country-wide business might. If in doubt, get a second opinion.

Although a consultant can be expensive – perhaps doubling the price of your computer system – the long-term benefits could justify the initial outlay. If your computer is vital to the efficient running of your business and you are unsure of your own technical abilities then a consultant can be a very cost-effective option.

Buying from a dealer

Buying from a dealer can be a risk. Computer dealers range from small shops run by enthusiasts to large multinational companies. They also vary widely in terms of quality of service, reliability, professionalism and support. The ideal is a friendly local dealer who has a strong interest in retaining your business, enjoys working in the trade and has plenty of experience to draw on.

Unfortunately, some dealers are less than scrupulous – it is no exaggeration to say that a handful are little more than used-car salesmen who, aware of the potential of a new market, have been quick to take advantage of it. If you fall foul of one of these you can find yourself being deliberately misled by someone who wants to off-load obsolete stock at an inflated price and has no interest in your needs or long-term custom.

To ascertain whether you are dealing with a saint or a shark simply visit your local dealer in person, explain roughly what you are looking for and listen closely to the response. Vague sales pitches such as 'This is the very best', 'Everybody uses this one' or 'Really fast machines, these' should be treated with suspicion. Try applying the same criteria as you would when assessing a consultant. Does there seem to be a genuine understanding of what your needs are? Is there a wide range of options to choose from, or are you being steered towards stock that is piled high in the shop front? Does the shop assistant demonstrate knowledge of the subject and a professional attitude? If you feel confident about the level of aptitude and service then you have probably found your source. You may pay more in the beginning this way, but you may also find yourself with a free source of help and advice – both of which can be invaluable for inexperienced users.

If you are unable to find a good local dealer, you have the option of buying by mail-order from computer magazines. Take the same approach again – telephone the computer company, talk to the sales department, explain what you want, ask a few awkward questions and note down the replies. The tone, precision and usefulness of the responses will tell you a lot about the way that particular dealer does business. You cannot realistically expect the same level of service from a mail-order dealer – especially a large one – as you would from a small local shop.

It is tacitly acknowledged in the industry that the high-street consumer electronics stores are likely to offer you the worst of both worlds. Prices are often significantly higher than elsewhere, and the level of support and help that the staff can offer tends to be minimal. At best you may be steered towards big-name products that happen to be in stock at the time. At worst you may find that you know more about the computers than the staff on the other side of the counter. Some high-street retailers offer telephone support – at a price. If you want help – and you will need it if you are new to computers – you will probably be asked to pay for it by the minute on an 0891 number. This can be stressful and expensive, and you have no guarantee that your problem will be solved.

High-street stores often charge a much higher annual percentage rate (APR) than a bank or other credit source might. As a result, you can find yourself spending the kind of sums that might have bought you the services of a consultant, yet you could still be left with something that you cannot use properly, which does not quite do the job you want, and which you do not understand.

Do it yourself

Doing the background research and buying a computer yourself is the most time-consuming option and the most demanding in terms of your personal resources. Buying a computer 'blind' with no research at all is very unlikely to get you a good deal. In fact, it may not even get you something you can use effectively.

If you have the time, it can be worth learning the basics of the subject from the hundreds of books, magazines and courses that are available. This can be a good investment as dealers tend to respect knowledgeable customers more than complete novices. The difficulty is that not everyone has the time, inclination, interest or mental aptitude needed to master the field.

This approach can only be recommended if you are not in a hurry, if your computer is not going to be central to the running of your business and if you feel you have the abilities to take on the subject in depth. The rewards can be high, however. You will be able to save on hardware costs, because you will know how and what to buy and at a much lower price. You will also be less dependent on outside help. Just like someone who knows how to repair his or her own car, you can enjoy the benefits of cost-saving and independence. The disadvantage is that it takes time to learn all you need to know to reach this standard.

Buying second-hand

At first sight, the second-hand approach may seem appealing for several reasons. You will be buying a tried-and-tested system which someone else has already been using. In theory all the teething troubles should have been sorted out, and you will be able to work with something that does the job straight away.

However, there are a few caveats. It is important to remember that computer equipment depreciates quickly. This means that second-hand 'bargains' are rarely what they appear and, in many cases, you will be able to buy a new, much better system for the same price as a second-hand one.

Another problem is that for legal reasons software cannot usually be sold to a third party, even when it has been paid for in full by the original owner. This means you will not be eligible for any help the manufacturer may offer to users, and you will not be able to take advantage of any improved versions (**upgrades**) of the software that the manufacturer decides to release, unless you buy them at the full price.

Finally, you cannot be sure that someone else's system matches your needs. Their set-up may be perfect for them, but it may not be right for you.

Second-hand computer equipment does have its uses, though. If you are working to a very tight budget – a few hundred pounds, perhaps – then you will have to buy second-hand. In this part of the market the equipment has depreciated as much as it is going to, making it less of a long-term risk, but there are still pitfalls to watch for. The most worrying is that spare parts and consumables may no longer be available. Before buying, check that you can still get these for the second-hand machine. For example, some models of the Amstrad word processor family of small computers use a special kind of plastic diskette to store information. These are no longer widely available. If you can find a source locally or perhaps buy up a large stock from somewhere else, you will find that these machines offer good value for simple word-processing and accounting tasks. Without a source of these consumables, however, they are only slightly more useful than a doorstop.

With a little help from your friends

In theory this is the best and cheapest way to get help. In practice, you should make absolutely sure that your friends and colleagues fully understand your computer requirements and have set up a similar system for themselves before you act on their advice. Unless you have a friend who is prepared to help you put a system together from start to finish, you should treat the advice of friends and colleagues as a source of useful, but not definitive, information.

New is not always best

Innovation is a permanent feature of the computer industry. If you are doing your own research and making your own purchasing decisions you may encounter **advance product announcements**. The product may look worth waiting for but as a rule of thumb it is best not to wait. *Be wary of any major innovation.* If a product has been on sale for less than a year and a half there is still a chance that there may be something wrong with it. Many new products simply are not reliable. This may sound incredible, but time and again this has proved to be the case. Manufacturers of both hardware and software are under great pressure to keep ahead of their competitors and products are often released before they have been fully tested in the field. If your computer needs are conservative and you need reliability far more than the very latest, fastest and best of everything then it is prudent to avoid becoming a manufacturer's guinea-pig.

If you do need the very latest and best – and particularly if you are likely to lose work to your competitors without it – then you may need to take the risk. This can put you in a more vulnerable position than someone who is buying established technology. To minimise your risk, hold out as long as you can and watch for any problem reports in computer magazines.

Another reason to avoid waiting for new products is because sometimes they simply fail to appear: this phenomenon is known as **vapourware**.

A typical piece of vapourware is announced; it misses its first release date, its second, and perhaps even its third and fourth. A year or more may have passed since the first announcement. Sometimes vapourware does eventually appear as a genuine product, but not invariably. There is no way of knowing in advance how it will turn out.

Computer manufacturers have been known to use colourful and creative tactics to put the competition at a disadvantage. Advance product announcements are among these.

Manufacturer A is about to release an impressive new product. Manufacturer B, whose sales will be hurt by this, hears about the new product and immediately announces to the world that brand-new B product is better and will be available very soon. Some buyers wait for product B. The release date comes and goes. Manufacturer B announces that there are a few problems. However, not only are these being sorted out, but the extra time is being used to incorporate some exciting new features. The second release date passes. Buyers are now confused – should they buy product A, which is known to work and is available now, or product B which sounds much more impressive but is not yet available?

A product that you can use now is worth more to you than one that is not yet available – no matter what claims are being made for it. As a small business or home user your needs are modest and you can safely ignore the scheming, plotting and salesmanship. If in doubt, get something that is known to work. If it does what you want, and you are confident you will be comfortable using it, then buy it. If something better comes out later you can always change it – if you still need to.

GREAT EXPECTATIONS?

However you buy your computer, assume that you will not be able to work with it straight away. The software and the hardware both require a learning curve – a period of time which you will need to familiarise yourself with the system.

It is a good idea to start with simpler software, such as a word processor, to gain basic experience and confidence before moving on to more complicated packages.

CHAPTER 3

PRESENTATION, DTP AND GRAPHICS

THE QUALITY and visual appeal of your stationery can tell those with whom you correspond a lot about your business. With a computer it is possible to produce print-shop-quality results at a fraction of the price. The production of letters, diagrams and leaflets can be streamlined so that they can be created to order much more quickly. What follows is an introduction to the possibilities offered by computer-based word processing, desktop publishing and presentation software.

Basic word processing

Why use a word processor when a typewriter will do? If you have been using a typewriter for many years without problems, why pay the extra for a word-processing system? For some kinds of work a typewriter is still perfectly adequate: a cheap, reliable way to produce high-quality letters. For something more versatile, however, it is worth considering a computer-based word-processing system.

The chief advantage of electronic systems is that you can correct mistakes before you print them. You can make as many changes as you like in the document before the print touches the paper. Paragraphs are managed automatically. If you delete a word in a sentence the remaining words move to fill in the gap.

Word processing also gives a range of broader editing options. Words, sentences and paragraphs can be moved around. Text can be copied from one document to another. Footnotes and headers can be added and pages can be numbered automatically. You can also keep electronic copies of your work, so that letters can be stored inside the computer or on floppy discs and re-used later with minor changes. It is also possible to build up a library of blank letter headings addressed to different clients which will save typing in their details every time.

A very useful word-processor feature which has been available for some time is the **mail merge facility**. Mail merge works by taking a standard letter with carefully ordered blanks, and then filling in the details from a separate list. It can also be used to print envelopes. It is possible to include simple individual details which can make a letter look more personal.

Layout

At the next level of sophistication a word processor gives you detailed control over the visual appearance and layout of the text. Lettering has always been available in different styles (called **fonts**) and sizes (measured in **points**). Most word processors are supplied with a selection of basic fonts. Extra fonts are available as libraries, almost always at additional cost. The main text of this book is typeset using a font called Bembo with letters that are 10½ points in size. Other examples of fonts and point sizes include:

This is 9 point Times Roman

This is 12 point Courier

This is 14 point Helvetica

This is 15 point Century Schoolbook

Fonts can add extra impact to a piece of work when used with restraint and discretion. For letter-writing it is more practical to use one font, although you may want to add a letterhead in a different style to make the letter more eye-catching. The addition of **font styles**, such as **bold** or *italic* can emphasise points in the text and make headings distinctive. Underlined, superscript, and subscript lettering can also be used.

For example, a standard letter could be improved by using different lettering styles and sizes: the name and address of both the sender and the recipient could be in bold text, and the name of the signatory could be underlined. All of these details could be stored in the computer with the text of the standard letter.

Professional word-processing software includes a set of style sheets for applications such as memos, faxes, business letters and presentations. These contain no text, only the information needed to lay out the different areas of text on the page. They are easy to use and excellent results are possible.

Spelling and grammar checkers

Spell check is a facility on most word processors. It scans a document and queries unusual words. Most have a dictionary option so that you can add words of your own. Spell checkers are invaluable but not infallible. They have no way of noting common mistakes, such as misspelling 'their' or 'there' for 'they're', where the words arc spelled correctly but the proper use depends on context.

It is important that you get a checker with an English dictionary. Early examples used American spellings ('color' for 'colour', and so on) and these proved more of a hindrance than a help for UK users. Most professional packages on sale in the UK now include UK spellings but if you buy a cheaper package it is a good idea to check this.

Many word processors also include a **thesaurus**. This works like the paper equivalent, except that it can benefit from the computer's speed and suggest alternatives more quickly. Computer-based spell checkers and thesauri are limited in the number of words they have in their vocabularies; most contain as many words as a small dictionary. A computer version of the *Oxford English Dictionary* is available – but it is expensive, and the current version does not integrate seamlessly with any of the popular professional word-processing packages.

Grammar checkers are more subtle and often less useful tools. A grammar checker scans a piece of text for grammatical errors, such as split infinitives and dangling participles. It gauges the impenetrability of the prose according to a variety of measures, one of which is estimated reading age. Grammar checkers are entertaining to play with and can offer some advice on how to improve writing style. However, the subtleties of the English language are still beyond the grasp of even the most powerful computer, and many of the suggested 'improvements' will be irrelevant, misleading or hilarious.

Outline managers and other text tools

Professional word processors also offer options which make the management of text much easier: for example, they can literally count the number of words in a document. Other information such as the creation date is also likely to be available.

Outline managers can transform a list of notes into a neatly laid out outline that can form the skeleton of a writing project. The word processor can prepare a contents list or an index, maintain a list of revisions, or keep track of a table of authorities for listing references in a legal or other professional context.

Macros

Most professional word processors include a **macro** facility. This provides an easy way to automate regularly repeated actions. A macro is a recorded set of actions that can be 'played' manually or automatically when you start using the word processor. If, for example, you want the last two documents you were working on to reappear on screen when you start up your word processor, you can create a macro that loads and displays them for you.

Macros can be as basic or as complicated as you care to make them. Most word processors are supplied with a range of macros that add extra features to the package. For example, the Lotus Word Pro word processor comes with around 200 macros that can be used for cross-referencing text, clearing the screen, finding old documents and so on.

CASE HISTORY: William

William Henley, who writes for a national magazine, recalls his first encounter with a powerful word processor.

'As a writer all I have to worry about is the text, and it's the production editor who looks after the layouts and the graphics. But even basic editing has been made a million times easier with a word processor; it's really useful to be able to go back and rewrite and add to work after it's been typed in.

'We have contributors who supply their work on disks. One problem is the number of different formats, so we ask for plain uncoded text – known as ASCII [American Standard Code for Information Interchange] – which is the lowest common denominator and doesn't include extras like italics, but will work on any system. Even then we get compatibility problems. Sometimes there are strange characters at the start of each paragraph and so on.

'To sort this out I use a macro that goes through a document and deletes everything that isn't standard. I used to do this by hand, and it could take minutes to go through a piece and delete the stuff that wasn't wanted. Now it takes a few seconds. I have other macros which help with basic layouts, so I can produce copy that doesn't need much fiddling around with when it's laid out. And the word-count tool is a godsend. We have to write to length, and it makes that a whole lot easier.'

Desktop publishing

Whereas word processing is text-oriented and ideal for letters, memos and faxes, **desktop publishing (DTP)** is used whenever text and graphics have to be laid out on a page. Typical uses include newsletters, price lists, advertising flyers and posters.

DTP continues where top-end word processors leave off, by adding features such as the ability to split text between columns and pages, to make it flow around complicated shapes, to print it upside down, sideways, at an angle or along a curved line, and to include photographs and other images on the page. Font handling is much more sophisticated, making it easy to produce banner headlines, paragraph headings and quote boxes. Lines, ovals, boxes and frames can be added to draw attention to areas of text, and textures and borders can be created to make a document look more ornate. Unlike word-processing software, which is almost exclusively used to print black letters on white paper, all but the very cheapest DTP software can work with performs relatively well in Eastern Europe. As for price, several of the top wines were relatively more expensive, but further down the score sheet there was not a clear price/quality correlation. Vintage also counted for little in the results.

The number of corked or faulty bottles was shockingly high – nine had to be replaced by second samples. This is exactly the number we had to retry at the last *WWM* Eastern European tasting, but we had fewer wines in this tasting, so it really did mark a new all-time low. Of the replacement bottles, three showed the same fault, three were much improved, and the panel was undecided on the others.

THE VERDICT

Tasters were horrified by the high number of faulty bottles, and, indeed, by the low standard of the wines in general. Although the top wines gained decent marks, the number of mediocre wines that fell into the 'average' and 'below average' categories was alarming.

'The cockroaches are certainly coming out of the cupboard . . .'

Among the more specific complaints were a lack of structure and balance; dilute – even 'watery' – wines; and a lack of varietal distinction. Fresh fruitiness was missing; tasters found too many wines where the fruit had been hard-pressed and stretched for flavour. And, to cap it all, there were many complaints of 'dirty wood' character.

Aileen Hall spoke for the entire panel when she wrote that 'corked bottles are one thing, but dirty wood is another - surely the supermarkets and other advisers should have helped these wineries clean up their act by now?' Jane Hughes predicted that at this rate the producers would lose their grip on the everyday drinking market: 'We treat Eastern Europe as a source of cheap party wines, but not many of these would even fit that bill.' Clive Patten agreed:

'On the basis of this tasting, Eastern Europe's position as a leading supplier of inexpensive red wine must be under threat.'

Andrew Jefford was equally condemning: 'Up until the very top price bracket in the tasting there was no point in buying any of these unless you're going to make mulled wine – a ropier series of wines I have never met before at a *WWM* tasting.'

It was left to Andrew Cotterill to point out that there were 'some good, easy-drinking, uncomplicated examples which, with their reasonable price tags, represent good value'. True, we had liked some of the wines, but they were the slightly more pricy bottles. 'There was a flurry of fuller and fruitier "new-style" wines at the more expensive end of the tasting,' Andrew Jefford agreed. As the tasting was blind, he added: 'Perhaps these were the ones made by outside interferers, be they flying winemakers or dictatorial supermarkets.' Well, no, as it turned out, they weren't. Our international interferers did not fare especially well in this tasting, as the individual comments that follow indicate. Still, 'sourcing good wine in large quantities from Eastern Europe is very hard,' according to Andrew Cotterill whose job it is to do just that for Sainsbury's. 'We are constantly trying to isolate better parcels of wine, and most wineries are massively in debt.' Clive added: 'Winemakers are under intense pressure to supply vast amounts of wine – you can only squeeze so hard and then the pips pop!'

We are clearly witnessing a poor period in Eastern European winemaking, as hard-pressed producers realign their raw materials and adjust to the climate of change. After the past two vintages of cheap wine from Iberia and the south of France, Eastern Europe cannot afford to take our allegiance for granted any more – especially to such inconsistent quality. A final word from Andrew

This text from *Which? Wine Monthly* was created and edited using a word-processing package called WordPerfect 5.1 and laid out using DTP software called PageMaker colour although you will need access to a colour printer to print out the results.

Even a budget DTP package is capable of far more striking results than a word processor. The two are often used together, with the latter providing basic text-editing features and the former more sophisticated page layout facilities. Most DTP software includes filters which can import text directly from a range of popular word-processing packages. This ensures that special effects such as italics are maintained.

Graphics can be imported in a similar way. These can be clip art (examples above) or graphs or tables that have been created using other software. (Clip art is a selection of basic cartoons, images, drawings and sketches that is often supplied with a DTP package. As with fonts, extra images are available at additional cost.)

CASE HISTORY: Jessica

Jessica Macbeth is a teacher and personal skills trainer who also works as a writer. She uses her DTP system to produce limited editions of books which she sells at her classes.

'I use a laptop computer with Adobe PageMaker DTP software to work on my books. I also have a scanner and a cheapish bubble-jet printer. You can get books of clip art with all kinds of different images, and I scan these in and use them to add spice to my work.

'For the page layouts, I have about 50 different fonts installed, although I tend to use the same handful again and again. They have a huge effect on the look of a page.

'The results I get when I print them out are good enough to take to a printer. He scans in the pages and prints them out using a professional printing press. I supply the artwork double-sized, and he reduces it. This *reduction takes away some of the rougher edges. For my next project I've found a printer who can take my disk directly.*

'*It's a lot of fun and very satisfying too. Anyone who has basic layout skills can do it. This is what DTP was supposed to be about, before it was hijacked by the corporate world. It doesn't have to be used for business reports; people can have fun with it too.*'

Hypertext and multimedia

Today, most documents are produced on paper. However, for some users words and graphics are not enough. Many top-end word processors now include a facility which allows sound and video clips to be added. These documents can only be viewed on another suitably equipped computer. These multimedia documents are an indication of how information will be exchanged in the future, when words, sounds, pictures, video clips and other kinds of information will be integrated seamlessly.

Multimedia documents lend themselves to the creation of **hypertext**, which does not follow the traditional linear format of the printed page. A typical hypertext document includes areas of the screen that respond to the user's enquiries. Some words may be highlighted: when selected, further information on the topic in question is revealed. These 'hidden' pages may contain links of their own, and so on. The result is an 'intelligent' document that can be browsed through, following words and ideas that take your interest, rather than as a linear sequence of words that has to be read from start to finish.

One application of hypertext is the electronic CV (curriculum vitae), which has proved popular in creative fields such as advertising and design. As well as plain text, an electronic CV can include voice clips, photographs, examples of previous work and snatches of music. This lends itself to all kinds of intriguing creative possibilities.

A more mundane application of hypertext is the creation of computer-based help for computer-users, which is rapidly becoming the standard for new software. Users are presented with a list of basic options, from which they select the 'help' option. From here, they can explore different topics in more detail. Because these are linked to each other in an intelligent way, there will always be a list of relevant options available on screen at any point in the process.

Some companies in the United States now present their annual reports as a hypertext document which is distributed on CD and includes video clips of the directors and animations showing the financial results. The non-linear nature of hypertext makes it easy for investors to access the information they want.

A company called Adobe is also pioneering their Acrobat system, which is a computer-independent way of presenting electronic documents. The Acrobat reader software is available free, and allows users of any kind of computer to read documents prepared with the Acrobat system, which can contain text, graphics and other information. Acrobat is an indication of the likely direction of electronic publishing in the medium term.

Apple computer-users have had access to a hypertext product known as Hypercard since the late 1980s. IBM-compatible users have access to OLE (Object Linking and Embedding), which was developed by the Microsoft Corporation. Both of these products can handle the demands of a full hypertext system. OLE takes hypertext a stage further by including links between applications, as well as information. Because all the links are maintained automatically it is possible for different people to contribute to the same document. One person can be responsible for graphics, another for text and a third for sound. They can work independently, but whenever one person makes a change the document as a whole is updated. OpenDoc (Open Document) a new proposal from Apple takes this idea further still. (For more information see Appendix III.)

Business presentations

Presentations have become an accepted part of the business scene over the last few years, whether to ask a bank for money, pitch for business or investment, or to pass on information within a company.

Computers can play a major role in the preparation of a presentation. Apart from word processing and DTP for the production of high-quality handouts and slides, there is a set of tools specially developed for presentations. These packages are geared to the creation of punchy images with banners, slogans and other details. Most of these can support graphs, charts, video-like animations, such as cuts and crossfades between pages, sound effects and video clips, as well as straight text.

Like word processors, most packages include templates which make it easy to build a complete presentation. They also contain libraries of backgrounds, foregrounds, clip art and other graphics which can be used to customise the presentation. A complete beginner can produce a professional presentation within a day or so; experienced users can do the same much more quickly.

You can make presentations directly from your computer. A useful, if expensive, option is the overhead projector screen. This plugs into the back of your computer and fits over a standard overhead projector base. The screen is translucent, and whatever appears on it is projected in the usual way. As a result, you can prepare a presentation on your computer, and then project it to your audience while controlling the presentation from your computer's keyboard. Remote control options are also available, allowing you to walk around the room and make your presentation at the same time.

Portable computers, discussed in Chapter 9 and Appendix VII, are often used for this purpose. These allow you to add full hypertext links to a document. With the addition of some speakers, or access to a small PA system, you can use your computer to create a full sound and video experience.

Pre-printed paper

Unless you work with hypertext, text and pictures are designed to be printed.

To be able to do justice to the physical appearance of any work you produce you need to use the right kind of printer (see Appendix II). Even with a cheap printer there are things you can do to make your work more attractive.

CASE HISTORY: Isabel

Isabel Davis, who works for a firm of accountants, was given the job of producing an information pack for new clients. She considered using printed colour brochures designed on a DTP system, but discovered there was a cheaper way to create a similar effect.

'Someone sent us a catalogue of pre-printed papers, and I was very impressed. They come in a huge selection of colours and designs, and some even come with templates you can use with your existing software.

'I sent off for some samples and decided on a basic style, which is available for various formats — business cards, letterheads, presentation covers and so on. I used the DTP system we have to add some fancy lettering, and saved that as a letterhead. Now, whenever anyone prints a document, the heading appears at the top, fitted into a blank space on the special paper. It looks very eye-catching.

'People have started to look at us as a dynamic company that gets things done, so we've had quite a bit of extra business.'

Pre-printed paper is available from specialist outlets (see Addresses). At its simplest it can be used as a striking background for posters and other displays. Commercially produced paper that is designed specifically to be used in a business setting — folded flyers, letterheads, business cards and compliments slips — is not customised: areas are left blank so that details of individual businesses can be added. Some companies also supply templates which can be used with the most popular word processors. This makes it even easier to design high-quality output on-screen, before committing it to paper, and at a very low cost.

For some kinds of work, however, only the very highest quality is acceptable. High-quality colour printers are available for around £3,000. These will come down in price over the next few years, but at the moment are out of reach of all but businesses with a substantial colour printing requirement.

Print bureaux

Print bureaux can take text and graphics created on the computer and print them on commercial-scale machines. One possible application is the creation of slides for a business presentation. You design these at home or at the office and then give the information on disk to a print bureau. The bureau will turn this into pin-sharp slides which can be used in the normal way. Your local print shop may already offer this service. If not, you can find details in *Yellow Pages*.

Voice dictation systems

A recent development in the word-processor market is the voice dictation system. Instead of typing your words, you speak them into a microphone. You can make words appear on the screen and to a limited extent you can also control your computer this way.

Current voice-based systems suffer from a limited vocabulary and you have to insert small pauses – around one-fifth of a second – between words. They can recognise up to 120,000 words, which is adequate for technical, legal or medical applications, and vocabularies are growing. Continuous speech

---

PACKAGES TO WATCH FOR

The word-processing market is dominated by Microsoft Word, Lotus Word Pro and Corel's WordPerfect. Each of these packages offers a huge range of features and can be used for almost anything. Word Pro is only available for the PC. For Apple Mac users comparable packages are Mac Write Pro and Nisus. Personal preference will dictate your choice.

DTP is dominated at the budget end of the market by Microsoft's Publisher, which is powerful but extremely easy to use, and includes hints and sample page layouts to get you started. At the top end, the choice is between Quark XPress and Adobe PageMaker. PageMaker is the original DTP package, but Quark XPress is used by many magazine companies and publishing houses. Both include a full complement of professional features.

For presentations Lotus' Freelance is very quick and easy to use, even by a complete beginner, and includes a huge collection of backgrounds and page styles.

---

dictation systems are a couple of years away. At the moment, the systems have a recognition speed of around 40 words a minute. Most systems need to be trained to recognise a voice; some do this on a continuous basis and become more accurate with use. Dictation systems are available on the PC from IBM and a company called Dragon Dictation Systems, and on the Apple from Articulate Systems.

CHAPTER 4

KEEPING TRACK OF YOUR MONEY

REPETITIVE and tedious chores such as accounting, bookkeeping and VAT are perfect tasks for a computer. It will make the dull jobs easier, thus saving you time, and it can help you be more organised.

CASE HISTORY: Ray

Ray Thomas recently decided to computerise his business, a garage and used-car dealership, having found that keeping up with PAYE, tax, VAT, billing and other financial matters was getting beyond him.

'We were just coming out of the recession. We'd survived pretty well and I'd kept all my mechanics. Business was picking up again, but I was spending more time on paperwork than I wanted. I used to employ someone to come in and do the books and sort out everyone's pay at the end of the month. But he retired, and getting anyone else in would have been costly. I started to wonder whether a computer might help me out.'

Ray was able to get help by asking his local TEC [Training and Enterprise Council] for details of someone who could put a system together for him. They also suggested he went to the local college to get some basic training.

'I was worried about this, but it wasn't nearly as bad as I thought. It took a while to work out what was what, but by the end of the course I'd got the basics under my belt. The TEC also suggested some names of people who could help me out. We bought the kit from a local firm, and they've been really good about the problems we've had – but there haven't been many. Gary, one of the mechanics who knows a bit about *computers, sorted out the software side of things with a bit of help from them. And now it works like a dream. The computer does everything my old accountant used to do. It looks after the VAT returns, works out all the PAYE deductions – and so on. It even prints the cheques. We use stationery that works with the software. When the tax codes change and allowances change, Gary just keys in the new ones. It takes a couple of hours, and we're set for another year.*

'Gary suggested doing some leaflets on the computer. It hardly cost us anything because he used some software that came free with a magazine. And when we did a leaflet run locally it got us some new trade.

'All told I think the system cost about £2,000 to set up. Now that's a one-off payment, but we were paying the accountant more than that each year. I'm thinking of opening a car-hire business now, so we've started working out how the computer can help with that too.'

Buying financial software

There is no lack of suitable software for managing money, as the advertisements in computer magazines show. Many excellent packages are available at very reasonable prices, and unless you are running a very large business you should be able to pick up a system that does everything you need for £500 – much less if you are a sole trader.

Most **accounting packages** contain a minimum of purchase ledger support, sales ledger support with account tracking (so you can watch for late payments), cashbook calculations to look after petty cash and double-check bank statements, VAT tracking, balance sheets and profit-and-loss reports, and support for multiple bank accounts. An important feature is error correction – if you discover a mistake you should be able to correct it without having to retype every entry. Security may also be important, and some packages include password access. They may also offer the facility to design individual invoices, as well as support for different kinds of invoice (pro-forma, quotation and so on). One useful feature is the ability to set up discounts for individual clients.

As well as keeping track of employees, their hours and their payment schedules, **payroll software** should also cope with special circumstances such as one-off contracts, sick pay and maternity leave. It should be possible to set up regular payment schedules – weekly, monthly, four-weekly and annual – and rearrange these to deal with variable hours and payment rates. Good support for overtime calculations is essential. Some packages can deal with National Insurance (NI) payments for directors and the way in which company cars can affect NI and tax. You should also be able to produce a single report of PAYE details for the Inland Revenue and print this information directly on to the relevant forms.

Stock control software is more specialised. Features to look for include advance warnings of low stock, tracking of the total value of different items and a report of the total value of the stock as a whole. The software should be capable of optimising stock levels as well as keeping track of them; a range of simple analysis options and reports will help you with this. Useful extra features include the capacity to add additional information to the stock description of each item, so, for example, items which need to be sold together can be flagged as such at the counter, and a measure of the amount of warehouse space taken by different stocks.

Some packages are tailored to the needs of specific businesses. These are advertised in trade journals and offer a comprehensive all-in-one solution for the typical small business user. They tend to be more expensive than off-the-shelf products and can also be less flexible. On the other hand, they are written specifically for a certain market and incorporate terms and concepts with which that market is already familiar. Such packages do one kind of job very well indeed and require less setting up. In general, however, standard business packages can do the same kind of work for less money.

As with other products, it is useful to check for specific features when deciding which software to buy. With financial products watch out for the following:

Ease of use Software should not be hard to use. There is no need to follow the conventions of accountancy – such as double-entry bookkeeping – if you find these confusing and they do not fit your requirements.

Professional recommendations A product that is recommended by an official body, such as the Institute of Chartered

Accountants, or the Inland Revenue and HM Customs & Excise, is more likely to be productive. The Inland Revenue will accept direct printouts from certain brands of software which will not require the further services of an accountant.

Printing facilities and stationery Some packages offer their own printed stationery, including cheques and invoice forms. Others support stationery from other sources, such as printed P35 annual returns. Since it is your computer's job to save you time, the more pre-printed stationery you can buy, the better. Otherwise you may be left with software that produces results on the screen, but leaves you to write out 200 cheques by hand at the end of the month. Check which stationery you can use, how much it costs and how easily you can get hold of it.

Features Most of the common accounts packages offer all the basics you need. However, if you run a medium-sized business that trades overseas and has many different bank accounts you will need to check for extras such as multi-currency support and cross-account calculation options. In general, it is advisable to make a checklist of tasks – for example, maternity leave for PAYE calculations – and ensure that your software supports all of these. Good software will also offer further options; for example, support for BACS (Bankers' Automated Clearing Service), which can pay money straight into a recipient's account (see below).

When checking features, make sure you ask what kinds of reports are available. As well as a balance sheet and a profit-and-loss statement, you will also need to be able to track customer accounts, flag late payments and track creditor payments. As before, you should assess your needs carefully and make sure that the software can produce all the reports you need.

Support As with all software, you should check to see what kind of support the manufacturer or main distributor offers. Will you be able to telephone with queries if you get into difficulties?

Price Some sophisticated financial packages cost thousands of pounds. These are aimed at finance professionals and larger businesses and may not be ideal for the smaller trader. You should be able to get a very good package for much less than this.

Options Some packages integrate with other software from the same manufacturer and make it easy for you to share information between them. Some features – such as tax returns, invoice-tracking and financial analysis – are available as options. Make sure you get details of every product each manufacturer offers, so you can plan ahead for options. For example, you may not need to worry about VAT now, but if the business takes off you may be forced to start including this in your bookkeeping. It is always a good idea to plan ahead and get software that can cope with anything that might happen.

Updates Some financial software is available with an annual update option which contains the latest information on tax codes, allowances and other details. You can add this information yourself, but if your time is valuable it is worth checking to see if your software includes these updates.

Personal finance

There are a number of financial packages aimed specifically at the home user. These include features such as:

- bank statement reconciliation
- mortgage- and loan-planning
- credit card reconciliation
- bill-minding
- budgeting
- calculating expenses by category
- simple investment management
- overall net worth calculations.

These packages are recommended if you like to keep a tight rein on your finances and oversee exactly how your money is being spent. They are also an efficient way to check for bank and credit card errors.

For sole traders with a modest turnover, a personal money manager can be an excellent alternative to a larger accounts package. It will handle all the information you need to keep track of your income and expenses. The latter can be itemised according to category, so you can keep track of your spending and produce a single printout at the end of the tax year with all your expenses shown in detail. Categories are user-defined, so you can go into as much or as little detail as you like, and you may be able to supply the printout as part of your tax return.

Sophisticated money managers allow the user to track late payments and list when creditors should be paid. Some can even handle VAT, usually on the accrual system, which means that VAT becomes due when an invoice is issued, not when payment is received.

If your business needs are modest, it is a very good idea to look at these personal finance packages first rather than the larger business accounts packages. Many of the former include business-ready features such as invoice-tracking and VAT calculations. They are easier to set up and use than their larger siblings, and are often less intimidating to work with – which means you are more likely to take the time to keep your finances up to date. They may well be cheaper too.

For domestic use, these packages can take quite a bit of your time. To keep an accurate record you have to make each transaction twice – once in the real world and once in your computer. Given that many people use standing orders, direct debits, automated credits, debit cards, credit cards, cheques and cash to move their money around you might find that the time you need to spend to maintain an accurate picture is not worth it. This is something that depends on personal preference – some people like to keep track of every last penny, while others have an instinct for how much it is safe to spend and when, and are not concerned about the details.

Perhaps the most useful features of a personal money manager are bill management, loan estimation and cheque-book reconciliation. With accurate financial records it is easy to work out which bills are due and how much they are likely to be. This can give you warning of cash flow hiccups. Cheque-book reconciliation checks the figures in case your bank has made a mistake. Loan estimation can help you work out interest payments in unusual situations not covered by loan agents' tables.

CASE HISTORY: Terry and Sarah

Terry and Sarah McGinnes use a money manager to help them plan their long-term spending.

'We've been using it to work out whether or not we can afford to go on holiday somewhere exotic this year. Terry has been promised a salary rise, and we've been looking to see how that affects how much we can spend. He won't get the rise until we get back, so we're planning to take out a long-term loan now, and to pay it back more quickly than we would normally. We can get the loan because we can afford the monthly payments now, but it will cost us less when we pay it off quickly.'

Tax planners

A useful extension to the idea of the domestic money manager is the tax planner. These packages are updated every year and include all the details you need to fill in your tax return. The results can be printed on ordinary plain paper. Some packages have Inland Revenue approval for this, which means you can send in the sheet with a covering letter and do not need to copy the numbers across to your tax return form.

Tax planners can be a good way to estimate your tax liability, but they cannot give you the same level of advice as a trained accountant can. If your tax affairs are straightforward they can make the task of filling in your return much simpler. For the self-employed, some of whom will need to check whether specific expenses are deductible, it can be worth spending the money on hiring an accountant.

Portfolio managers

The management of stocks and shares is a task that is tailor-made for a computer. Not only can it keep track of prices, earnings and dividends, but it can also analyse market trends and make 'buy' or 'sell' suggestions based on proven analysis techniques.

It is perhaps surprising that there are not many investment management software packages. Personal finance managers include simple options which can allow you to keep track of your net worth, based on current stock prices. However, none of these packages includes any of the powerful predictive tools that professional brokers use.

The only widely available portfolio management system is made by Optimum Technology. It uses special hardware to link with the Teletext system to give instant access to the 'Teletext 2000' list of shares. It can also provide graphs and other market indicators. However, it does not keep track of the worth of your portfolio as a whole.

Shareware (see Chapter 8) is a good way to try out a range of low-cost investment managers. One of the best is PFROI, which offers a complete set of investment tracking and management functions including features such as valuation versus investment plots and portfolio totals. PFROI is available from the larger shareware libraries, along with a good range of other titles.

Spreadsheets

A spreadsheet is a general-purpose calculation tool. It provides a grid of cells that you can fill with information: a number, a date, a word or a formula. Most cells contain a number but they can also contain a formula that works with the numbers – a total, an average, a percentage and so on. The formulas can be simple or complex. Many spreadsheets are used as adding machines, providing a total for a set of figures in a column and then a grand total for the row of subtotals across the bottom. The range of possibilities is huge, however, and covers everything from simple arithmetic to complicated financial calculations such as loan repayment schedules, pricing based on profit margins, and useful figures such as the internal rate of return. Some spreadsheets include formulas to help with statistical analysis and engineering, and can handle general mathematical problems such as matrix manipulations and equation-solving.

The biggest advantage of a spreadsheet is the ease with which it can recalculate results. If one entry is changed in a column, the total at the bottom changes. No matter how complex or convoluted the calculations, the spreadsheet will keep track of

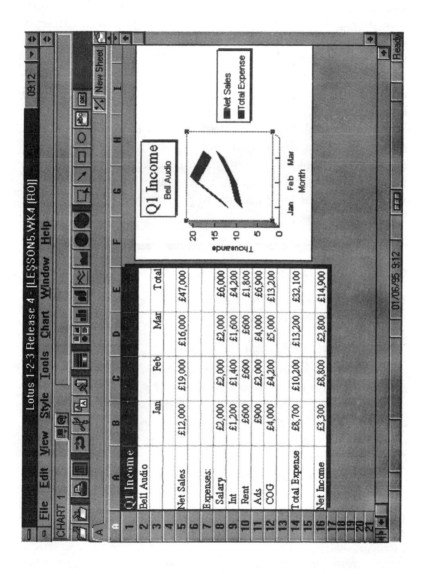

An example of a spreadsheet created using Lotus 1-2-3.

all the links between the numbers and formulas entered and work out the final result.

If you decide you need a spreadsheet, it is a good idea to look first at those included as part of an 'office suite'. These all-in-one packages include a spreadsheet, word processor, database and other optional extras such as presentation software and perhaps a personal information manager or a contact manager. A suite-based spreadsheet gives you *integration* between these different programs, so that information can be exchanged between them all quickly and easily.

Many spreadsheets can present information graphically. Pie charts, bar charts, line graphs and maps are all common. So, for example, you could prepare the financial aspects of a business plan in a spreadsheet, and then transfer the graphs and tables over to a word processor or DTP package to present them professionally.

CASE HISTORY: Laurie

Laurie Leonard used a spreadsheet to help him create a business plan for his new business and was able to use some of the more advanced features to good effect.

'I started off knowing nothing about business plans and less about accountancy, but after reading a few books I started to get an idea of what my bank manager was going to ask me when I asked for the loan.

'The best thing about the spreadsheet I used was the way that many of the measures I had to calculate, like gearing and the internal rate of return, were already included as formulas. It was easy to estimate sales figures, guess interest rates, work out loan repayments and so on. I could also play with the numbers to see what would happen if interest rates suddenly went up.

'I did a printout of the results, and took along my portable computer as well. Because of the "what-if" features I was ready for the difficult questions, and I got the computer to recalculate the new figures on the spot. I think my bank manager was impressed that I'd done my homework, and even more impressed at the built-in safety margins I was offering, and I got the loan I needed.'

Your money on-line

Many banks are now offering on-line services. These are not advertised widely, and counter staff and 'personal bankers' may not be aware of them. These services can be a useful way of keeping track of your money, especially out of normal business hours and can also save you time, by eliminating the need to make regular trips to your branch.

Each bank's system works the same way. You are given a special number for your modem to dial and software that manages the connection. Security is maintained with passwords, and in some cases you will also be given a secret personal identification number (PIN) and a 'smart card' (which is rather like a credit card), together with a reader you swipe the card through. Most systems include usage logs, so you can check for unauthorised access attempts.

At their most basic these systems give you a chance to check your balance and look at a recent mini-statement on screen. However, they are an expensive way to get this information and only start paying for themselves when you use them to transfer money from one place to another.

When you write a cheque you are charged a set fee. If you then post the cheque you will also have to pay postage, a couple of pence for the envelope, and someone's wages for the work.

With an on-line system you can avoid these expenses. You supply your bank with a list of recipients, including their bank account details and the sums to be paid. You send this information along the telephone line to your branch. The funds are then transferred at a nominal extra cost to you.

Below the level of 150 payments a month on-line banking systems will not be financially viable, although you may decide to use one anyway if you want the extra services outside office hours. Above this level it starts to make economic sense, as well as giving you the convenience of access to your funds outside normal hours.

There are two fund-transfer schemes operating in the UK: BACS and CHAPS. BACS offers an on-line cheque payment service. Instead of writing out a cheque, the details are supplied to the bank in some other way, but the transaction is treated as a cheque and suffers from the same delays. Unlike a cheque, however, the money is not *debited* from your account until it is transferred. BACS is ideal for payroll use, and with an on-line BACS system you can completely automate payroll payments and make all those end-of-month salary cheques redundant with a single phone call.

Some banks offer a simpler non-electronic version of BACS called BOBS (branch oriented BACS service) which works like a semi-automated standing order. You supply the bank with a list of people whom you pay regularly. Then once a month you supply a list of amounts to be paid to them. This can be presented as information on a floppy disk, as a computer printout or even as a handwritten slip. The bank then transfers the money according to your instructions. BOBS does not rely on modems and remote computer access, but it is slower and more cumbersome than purely electronic forms of transfer.

CHAPS (Clearing Houses' Automated Payment System) is a same-day version of BACS. CHAPS payment requests go directly to the inter-bank clearing network and are usually credited (and cleared) on the day the request is made. In effect, CHAPS offers an electronic banker's draft service.

Some on-line banking schemes also include options that allow payments to be made abroad. Most UK banks subscribe to the international SWIFT (Society for Worldwide International Financial Telecommunications) network. On-line payment requests can be routed through this network to move money out of the country. Some countries are not on the SWIFT network and payments made to these will be transferred by telex message. You may also come across TAPS (Trans-continental Automated Payment Service) which is another international network.

Access to the CHAPS, SWIFT and TAPS networks is useful for larger businesses that regularly trade abroad, and for anyone who needs to make guaranteed payments quickly. Most smaller businesses will not need to use these features. But for those that do access to on-line payments can give a competitive edge.

On the whole, all banks offer a similar selection of services across a comparable fee-scale. But some add extras which can make a choice easier. Barclays, for example, include options which give you details of current exchange and interest rates.

Others, such as the HOBS (Home and Office Banking Service) scheme from the Bank of Scotland, give you access to a special high-interest deposit account. By storing surplus funds in this account overnight you can gain extra interest.

FINANCIAL PACKAGES TO WATCH FOR

For the small business TAS Books (Megatech Software), Quick Books (Intuit), Sage Instant Accounts (Sage), Money Manager (Connect Software) and Pegasus Solo Accounting (Pegasus) are all excellent accounts packages. Many can be combined with extra modules to add features such as full reporting, job costing and so on.

For domestic users the most popular packages are Money (Microsoft), Quicken (Intuit) and Moneybox (MoneyBox Software).

Popular tax planners include QuickTax (Intuit) and the Consumers' Association's own tax-planning software, TaxCalc, which is updated anually.

The most widely used spreadsheets include the immensely powerful Lotus 1-2-3 (Lotus) and Excel (Microsoft).

CHAPTER **5**

KEEPING TRACK OF INFORMATION

SMALL BUSINESS courses traditionally emphasise the importance of bookkeeping and cash flow. But keeping track of information can be just as important to a business as keeping track of money. By using and storing information effectively you can benefit your business. For example, if you are dealing with hundreds of people, you can use your information store as a memory jogger to add personal details to the conversation, or you can keep track of what each conversation was about, and use the computer to remind you when another call is due. Computers excel at this kind of work and offer a much more efficient way of organising information than pen- and paper-based methods.

Personal information managers (PIMs)

A Personal Information Manager is a computer-based version of the popular ring-bound paper organiser. A typical PIM will offer you the following:

- an address book
- an appointment diary
- a 'to-do' list
- a year planner
- a space for general notes, useful tables and other information.

The computer-based PIM makes it a lot easier to keep the information up to date. Maintaining a list of addresses requires no messy alterations. When someone's address changes, you simply type in the new one (if you're likely to need the old one later you can always keep a safety copy).

Another very useful option is an **auto-dialler** feature. If you have a modem (an electronic phone-line link discussed in more detail in Chapter 7), some PIMs will automatically dial a telephone number for you. Support for dial prefixes (such as 9, for an external call through a switchboard, or 132 to access the Mercury network) is also provided. Unfortunately, this support can be rather basic. You will be able to specify your local STD code, so that local numbers are dialled without it, but usually Mercury users will need to keep track of local codes (which do not require the 132 code) by hand.

Another useful feature is the telephone log. Most organisers maintain a list of calls made using the auto-dialler. This can be helpful in estimating a telephone bill or in charging someone by the hour. Incoming calls can also be logged in a similar way, although this is a slightly more clumsy process, as the logging has to be started by hand when the call comes in.

Many PIMs include an alarm feature. You can set up your computer so it gives an audible reminder of an appointment before it happens.

The latest PIMs are beginning to include network-related features. (Networks are covered in Chapter 7.) This means everyone's appointments can be linked together. Team members can schedule appointments with their colleagues automatically, or you can use the network to find a time when everyone is free for a meeting. Another popular use is task assignment – a group manager can assign jobs to team members. The team leader can leave the fine points of the work to the team members and concentrate on scheduling a project as a whole.

CASE HISTORY: Kenneth

Kenneth Hesket discovered PIMs five years ago and has never regretted it.

'I got my PC way back when, and someone told me about a program called Sidekick. I tried it out and loved it right away. For the first time I could keep all my information organised in the PC and get at it in any way I could think of. I no longer keep a pile of scrap paper for addresses

*next to the phone. Now it all goes into the PIM. I've got into the habit
of using the "to-do" lists as a memory jogger and, all told, I get about
half as much again done now as I used to. I don't spend time looking for
things and I'm rarely late for appointments any more. It's one of the most
useful productivity aids I've ever come across.'*

Choosing a PIM

Some PIMs are simply electronic versions of paper organisers;
others take a much more free-form approach and let you
organise information as you wish. It is important to choose the
PIM that suits your way of working.

Here is a list of features to look for.

Flexibility You should be able to design your own address book
pages and specify what kind of information you want to include.
You may, for example, want to allow space for home and business
contact details for some clients, and perhaps electronic mail
addresses as well. Some PIMs are inflexible and the information
must be entered in a set way. Others are more open-ended, and
you can decide which details to include in the different sections.
An extreme example of this is InfoCentral, which can store any
kind of information and make any kind of connection between
each item.

Connections between sections If you enter an anniversary or
a birthday, it should appear in the diary section as well. Items put
into a 'to-do' list should also appear on the diary pages.

Display options You should be able to switch between one day
per page to at least one week per page.

Priorities You should be able to schedule tasks according to
priority. Tasks that are overdue should be flagged in some way
and carried over to the next day.

Specific dates As well as birthdays and other important dates,
you should also be able to specify dates such as 'the third

Wednesday in every month' or even just 'the 3rd of every month'. If the third happens to fall over a weekend then the PIM should warn you or move the date to the following Monday.

Alarms and tickles Alarms are to remind you of meetings. Tickles are reminders that a task is due for completion. You should be able to set the alarm to go off at a given time *before* an event.

Time logging Some PIMs include features to help you keep track of the time you have spent on different projects or talking to clients. Some of these can even produce a final billing record. Phone logs can be used to track both incoming and outgoing calls.

Search options PIMs tend to handle address information inflexibly. There is often not the option of setting up a company contact name and address and then listing other contact details, such as internal exchange numbers, for the people who work there. A search feature can work around this by giving a list of people who work for the company, even though their names and addresses may be scattered around your address book.

Security Some information in your PIM will be personal. Some you may need to share with colleagues and some may be changed by colleagues too, who may need to reschedule an appointment for you or add a task to your list. A PIM should include security features which control access to different areas. Most PIMs use a password system − one for you, one to grant *read only* access for colleagues and public access for those areas that are public and can be changed by anyone.

Communication features An auto-dialler is very useful if you have a modem. If you use e-mail, then e-mail address details will also be essential. Check also that the PIM can be organised to cope with multiple addresses.

Workgroup features These are most useful for sharing information within a team but redundant for those who work alone at home.

Speed and reliability The PIM should be able to get results quickly and reliably. It should have the capability to search for and present contact names quickly. Some PIMs may offer useful features, but if it takes minutes for the information to appear on screen you might as well be using a pen and paper.

PIMS to watch for

Lotus Organiser (Lotus Corporation) has scored consistently high marks in usability studies. It is very similar to a paper organiser but includes some simple linking, so that, for example, an entry in the 'to-do' list can call up a relevant telephone number. One drawback with Organiser can be that it is very structured, although some users find this reassuring as they can start using it right away. Version 2 adds network support but seems to be slightly slower. Version 1 is more useful if you are working on your own and may even be available at a discounted price.

Packrat (Action Computers) is a do-it-all PIM with more features than you could ever need. All information templates can be customised and there is full network support. Packrat also includes features which overlap with larger and more expensive project managers. It can even be integrated into other pieces of software, so that Packrat's options appear on screen when you are using your word processor or other software.

InfoCentral (Novell) is a different kind of PIM. Instead of the usual address book and calendar format, InfoCentral works more like an outliner. You can enter any kind of information and then build links between different items. This approach takes some getting used to, but users who make the effort to learn it are enthusiastic about what it can do for them.

Contact managers

PIMs tend to be calendar-oriented, with an address book section which is kept separate. Contact Managers (CMs) integrate these two kinds of information more closcly. If you need to keep track of the letters, faxes or memos you have sent to different people a CM is a better choice. A good CM can produce reminders when you need to get in touch with someone again, and can also produce personalised letters and faxes from the information you store in it. This can save you the task of typing out the same letter hundreds of times with only minor changes.

CMs can be very useful in a larger company which uses a computer network. The CM allows each department to share the same information, but in a different way. For example, if a customer calls technical support and is put through to sales, their details can be transferred at the same time and every aspect of the call can be logged. An advanced CM includes features such as sales forecasting, support for price lists, instant profit calculations, and 'meeting generators' for use on networks (you specify a list of attendees and the CM compiles a list of times that they are all free).

When choosing a CM you should look for the following:

Fax support Fax communications should be integrated seamlessly.

Network support You should at least be able to schedule meetings with colleagues on the network. Support for e-mail both inside and outside the company is another option.

History logging This is vital for a good CM. You should be able to log all your actions together with the responses they generate, and also be able to schedule reminders for yourself.

Document support and mail-merge These enable you to prepare standard letters, personalise them automatically and print them.

Query generation and reports You should be able to list information by company, by area and by any search criterion you choose. You should also be able to generate reports summarising your work.

Palmtop support Some CMs are designed to integrate well with palmtop computers. You can manage all your appointments on a big desktop computer, and then use the palmtop – traditionally a Hewlett Packard 95 – when out on the road. (For more information on palmtop computers and electronic organisers see Appendix VII.)

Databases

Databases are used to organise information in a user-defined way. They are powerful complex programs and can be used to extract summaries of information as well as keeping it together. Databases are completely open-ended, so you can organise your information in any way you like. You can also filter the information in different ways by presenting the database with a query. This produces a broad picture, known as a **report**, which conveniently summarises the facts and can help you spot trends, anomalies and other patterns. If, for example, you are maintaining a list of sales, you can create a report which totals the sales you have made to each customer. You could also total sales by geographical area, by specific towns, or even from all customers whose surnames begin with 'W'. It is this flexibility that makes databases so powerful and useful.

Basic databases allow you to keep track of any kind of information that can be represented as text or numbers such as

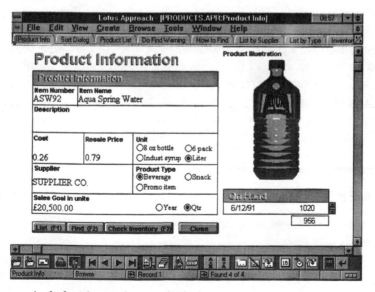

An example of a form design within a popular database

client contact details, sales records and so on. More advanced databases can also handle graphics – including photographs – and other kinds of information. There are two kinds of database:

Flatfile databases store information in a single table, and are more or less the computer equivalent of a card index. The 'cards' can be very complicated, with hundreds of entries on each one, but each card uses the same template for the information.

Relational databases spread information across different tables, while maintaining links between them, so you do not need to copy information unnecessarily. To understand this better, imagine a series of orders, each of which includes a customer's name and address. A flatfile database would require you to type in the name and address *for every single order received from that customer.* With a relational database you can assign each customer a number or code instead. The customer's details are kept in one place, and the order details make a reference to them. If the customer moves, you only have to type in the new address once. This is obviously quicker and more likely to be accurate than retyping the same information every time.

An important feature to look for when choosing a database is *referential integrity.* This means the software ensures that you never enter information without all the details filled in (e.g., you cannot create a purchase order without a set of customer details to go with it). Not all databases check for this, and without this feature you can experience problems as links between different kinds of information become confused.

Relational databases can be used for much more than maintaining names and addresses and keeping track of sales.

CASE HISTORY: Andrew

Andrew Kemble runs an advertising agency and uses a database to keep track of sales leads.

'We used to use a card index system and a set of diaries, and we had problems all the time. The system didn't work well if someone ran more

than one company, but had one account with us. That kind of thing caused confusion. Organising follow-up calls was a pain too. If someone was off sick we couldn't always make sense of what they'd written in their diary.

'We got someone to install a database for all this. Now we can search for people by their personal details, company name, or any other way. It's a lot easier to keep track of what they've used us for in the past. We can include details of the kind of work they've had from us in the past and build up a picture of what they'll be interested in in the future.

'But it's the follow-up calls that have really paid for the system. Now we just use the computer to print out a list of all the calls that need to be made that day. And it was a godsend last Christmas, it printed all our envelopes for Christmas cards.'

Database DIY

Unlike PIMs and CMs, databases need to be set up before you can use them. You have to decide what kind of information you want to keep and then create the templates (known as **forms**) needed to keep it. This can be a challenging task, especially for a beginner. Not only will you need to work through the software so that you understand what it does and how to use it, you will also need to think clearly about how to organise the information.

If your needs are fairly simple then form design will be obvious. Most database products include examples to help you and you should be able to modify these. Creating a more complex database, however, one which keeps track of sales, accounts and other information for a medium-sized company – is a job for a specialist programmer. Database design is one of the few instances where it will not be possible to buy something that is right for the job straight off the shelf.

Some databases include their own versions of a programming language, which is usually based on the popular BASIC (Beginners All-purpose Symbolic Instruction Code). This allows you to make detailed changes to information after it has been stored in the database.

CASE HISTORY: Mary

Mary Hardwick is network manager for a telesales company.

'My bosses were worried about Phoneday. We have tens of thousands of numbers in our system and it would have taken a team the best part of a week to make the changes by hand. But the database we use has a simple programming language, and I used it to write a program to check each number and change it appropriately. I wrote the program one morning, and by the afternoon all the numbers were ready for the big day. It was about as painless as it could be. I made a couple of mistakes, but we sorted those out well before the big switchover.'

This example illustrates the power of the database as an information management tool. It also shows that experience, skill and a natural talent for organising information are essential to get the best from this tool.

Choosing a database

In the same way that a spreadsheet is often sold as part of an 'office suite', databases are usually integrated with other products from the same manufacturer. It is possible to create your own collection of business applications from different manufacturers. However, this is a much more expensive option and makes it much harder to exchange information effectively between the different applications. Unfortunately, it is highly unlikely that you will be able to get hold of a demonstration version of a database from the larger manufacturers. Some databases are available as shareware but in the main you will need to rely heavily on reviews in computer magazines. Features of a database to consider include:

Ease of use Watch out for reviews that emphasise usability preferably with untrained or only slightly experienced users Read their comments to get an idea of how well you might do when trying to use the software. Older databases are text-based and these are harder to use. The latest examples allow you to design forms by moving boxes and other options around on the screen. These are much easier to use and usually produce better results too.

Flatfile or relational? The larger and more popular database packages are relational. You can use them as a flatfiler if you want to and explore the relational features later as you become more confident. You cannot work the other way, however. A flatfile system cannot be expanded to give you relational features. You will have more space and room for expansion with a relational database.

Form design options If you need to include photographs or graphics, ensure that the database can handle this. Some products include options to make forms look more appealing on screen, such as fonts and graphics which are purely decorative. Others take a much more workmanlike approach. If you need your forms to look good – and remember they can be printed, as well as appearing on screen – then check what kind of presentation control features you can use.

Speed Watch out for speed ratings (sometimes these are known as *benchmarks*). If you buy a slow database because it is easy to use but need access to thousands of records you may need to invest in hardware that is faster than average.

Hardware requirements Some databases are more demanding than others. Make sure that your computer has enough memory and disk space to be able to handle the database efficiently.

Help features Most modern software comes with help that you can access while working, so you will not need to refer to the manual once you have mastered the basics. But watch out also for templates and design hints to make your job easier, especially when you are just starting out.

Query features How easy is it to get information out of the database?

Do I need a database?

If all you need is a simple contact list then a PIM or a CM is a better – and cheaper – solution. However, if you need to do any of the following, a database will be more appropriate:

- include photographs and diagrams along with text and numbers
- create one-to-many links between information, and be able to list the details in different ways – for example, list all patients assigned to a certain doctor, or all patients taking medication bought from a certain company
- analyse information in many different ways – for example use sales figures to work out the most profitable product lines or geographical areas
- customise the way information is stored to suit your own special needs.

PACKAGES TO WATCH FOR

Microsoft's Access is currently the most popular and highly rated database product on the market. It includes cue cards which make it easy for you to design forms from scratch, even if you have minimal experience. Access is supplied as part of Microsoft's Office Professional Suite.

Lotus' Approach is another popular choice. This has also scored highly in usability ratings but also has a reputation for being slow when asked to deal with large amounts of information.

CHAPTER 6

EXCHANGING INFORMATION

If you are planning to use more than one computer, you should consider installing a network — a system that allows your computers to exchange information with each other and also to share printers and other facilities.

Networks

Networks come in three forms. The cheapest is known somewhat irreverently as 'sneakernet'. Sneakernet is not a true network. Information is transferred manually on floppy disks from one machine to another. This is time-consuming and disruptive and can result in more than one version of the same information. In an office where everyone is working on different parts of the same document, information needs to be carefully managed to prevent this. In spite of its disadvantages, 'sneakernet' is still used in some offices, where work is rarely shared and someone takes responsibility for preventing multiple versions.

Sneakernet works best if all the machines are the same type. It is now possible to transfer information between PCs and Macs quite easily. This was not always the case and if you have older machines you may be faced with compatibility problems.

The printer-sharing problem can be overcome with a **printer switch** that connects one of a group of computers to one or more printers. It is a simple and cheap solution. More complicated versions are available which can be switched remotely from the computer itself.

For groups of between five and twenty computers, the best option is the **peer-to-peer network**. This connects all the machines to each other. No one machine is more important than the rest – hence the 'peer' title. Each computer has a special 'public' area for information, and any computer on the network can read or write data to this area. This makes it ideal for situations where work needs to be passed from place to place. Security is maintained because only the public areas are shared. Private work can only be accessed from each individual machine.

A peer-to-peer network allows extras such as backup systems and printers to be shared between a group of users. Its biggest drawback is the disruption that can occur when new software is added to the system. The software has to be installed on each machine which can prove very time-consuming.

For larger work groups a **file-server system** is more efficient. This is built around a single central computer which serves as a repository of all the information in the company. The information on the server can be accessed by each satellite computer, which may or may not have its own hard disk, depending on the kind of work it is expected to do.

Server systems are complex and need to be installed by experts. They also require formal office organisation. A designated network manager ensures that the system runs smoothly and efficiently and that sensitive information is not available to all users.

Peer-to-peer networks and file-server systems rely on network cards – plug-in circuit cards that can link computers together – which need to be connected with a suitable cabling system. The details vary from system to system but a common standard is **Ethernet**, a reliable high-speed connection that can be used to link together all the computers in a large building.

Any network that is used exclusively by a single business is now becoming known as an **intranet**. In theory an intranet offers business users the kind of facilities available on the Internet (about which more later), but with a scope that is limited to the business itself. In other words, electronic mail and other information are passed freely from computer to computer within the company irrespective of whether the computers are in the same building or in different countries, but the information is disconnected from the rest of the Internet for security. A true Intranet is more efficient and secure than the Internet, but it is also more expensive to set up, especially for multinational companies. However, this new jargon word is now often used to describe any inter-office network, irrespective of the facilities it offers.

Network software

To get the most from a network you need to use the best possible software. Some software options become possible only once a network has been installed.

The biggest practical benefit of a network is **electronic mail (e-mail)**. Messages are typed on one computer and appear almost instantaneously on the screen of another. E-mail is an excellent way to improve office efficiency and is beginning to replace paper memos as the standard way of passing information between computer-users.

CASE HISTORY: Howard

Howard Hawker works as a programmer for a small company that produces computer games, and he found that the e-mail system was ideal for communicating with his colleagues.

'We use e-mail for a variety of things – to schedule meetings, pass on company news and deal with queries. It's a lot more immediate than typing a memo, but not as intrusive as making a phone call. People can read their e-mail when they feel like it, so it doesn't clamour for attention in the same way the phone does or interrupt concentration and work flow. It's helped our project to progress, and everyone seems to be getting a lot more done. Now I'm not sure I'd want to live without it.'

Networks are ideal for group management. Colleagues can contribute ideas and comment on projects without having to spend time in meetings. Some PIMs now include network-ready functions (see page 73).

A network is also an ideal tool for formal project management. Chapter 7 includes an introduction to project management software and many of the available software packages include integrated network features.

In a large company it is common for customer details to be stored in a single database that anyone can access. Customer correspondence, however, will usually still be scattered around different departments and it can take a whole morning of telephoning around to track down one letter.

Lotus Notes, a document database system, was designed to solve this problem by maintaining a list of all the relevant documents used in a company no matter in which department, building or site they are. The system is fully network-ready, so that if, for example, a customer sends a fax, the fax itself – with accompanying notes, if necessary – is stored in the database. In multi-site audit work, for example, different teams can build up a complete audit picture by using the package to integrate their individual contributions.

Lotus Notes is not a replacement for a conventional database; it lacks some of the advanced features these offer. Its great strength is that it is not limited to text. Any kind of information, including spreadsheets, graphics, sounds, images, fax messages and voice-mail messages can be maintained. Notes has proved successful and so far remains the only product of its kind.

The Internet

The three networks discussed so far have been Local Area Networks (LANs), limited to a single site. Wide Area Networks (WANs) offer the same kinds of facilities but across a much wider distance. Many WANs are owned and operated by companies, but one – the Internet – is open to anyone.

The Internet is a public-access network with some unusual features. No one owns the Internet, and there is no overall organising or administrative body. Instead, it works more as a loose affiliation of users, computer system managers, governments and commercial interests. It can be used to exchange information, software and mail between computer-users worldwide. Current estimates suggest the Internet is used by over 35 million users worldwide.

The public parts of the Internet have a very definite culture of their own, with their own vocabulary, ideas and social conventions. In these areas users debate issues, gossip and exchange information, often in quite a rough and ready manner. In other more professionally oriented areas the tone is more restrained. As a computer-user the latter areas can be most useful to you, as it is here that advice and computer support are exchanged.

To access the Internet you need a telephone and a modem. You can then open an account with an Internet Service Provider (see Appendix VIII for more details). You pay for this in much the same way that you pay for your existing telephone line, with a monthly subscription. In return you are given access to the Internet. Usually this access is via your modem over a telephone link – your computer dials the provider's computer, and a connection between the two is made. What happens next depends on the kind of service your provider offers. Some act as an electronic *poste restante*, collecting mail and other information for you, holding it until you dial in and then forwarding it to you along the telephone lines. Others act as a gateway that connects your computer directly to the Internet. This kind of connection is much more useful, but it can also be harder to set up and use. However, it is not necessarily any more expensive, and once it is up and running it can give you many more options and much better access to the services that the Internet offers.

Some service providers also charge you by the minute for any time spent using their services. A few, such as CompuServe, have a complicated pricing scheme where some services (such as access to certain stock-market prices) cost more per minute than others. There may also be extra charges for electronic mail on a per-message basis.

Access to the Internet offers a number of useful services:

Electronic mail (e-mail) Messages can be passed from computer to computer directly. Unlike network e-mail, however, the two computers can be anywhere in the world. If you are doing business abroad you can send a couple of pages of text overseas for far less than the cost of a telephone call or fax. You also have the benefit of knowing that your e-mail goes directly to your intended recipient. The transfer of mail is almost instantaneous. In extreme cases it may take an hour or two, but usually it arrives at its destination in minutes.

At the moment e-mail suffers from two drawbacks. It is best suited to plain text communications. It is possible to transfer sounds, pictures and even video clips electronically, but this can be an awkward, time-consuming and sometimes expensive process. As the technology of the Internet improves, these restrictions will lift, but for the next few years e-mail will remain a text-oriented system.

The second disadvantage, and for business purposes the greater, is that e-mail is not a secure way to communicate. There have been instances where e-mail messages were intercepted without the permission of either sender or recipient and used as evidence in court cases. To get around this e-mail can be **encrypted**. This turns the text into gibberish which makes no sense to anyone except the recipient who has a software key to unlock the original message. The best encryption system – PGP (Pretty Good Privacy) – is available as shareware. It can be slightly confusing to use, but once installed properly it offers near-total security.

Free access to software and other information A large number of software archives around the world offer unlimited free access to thousands of shareware and freeware software packages. Other kinds of information, such as current weather satellite images, recipes, travel information and hints and tips for almost every sport and hobby, are also widely available.

Free access to services which can help you find this information Knowing that the information is available is only part of the story. With the total number of computers on the Internet in the millions, it can be impossible to track down what you want without help. A number of free services (with colourful names like Gopher and Veronica) make this easier. These are fast 'intelligent' search tools that scan the Internet looking for information on a key word basis. A search based on the word 'mail', for example, would find a list of e-mail-related software and information, and supply you with details of the computers you would need to access to retrieve this data. There are also services which can help you find someone's e-mail address if you know the name and approximate location.

News groups These are the public discussion areas mentioned above. There are over 10,000 groups available and the numbers are increasing every day. They are arranged according to subject matter, which includes everything from computer topics to poodle-breeding and music fan clubs. Most service providers only supply a selection of the more popular and useful English language groups. The computer-oriented groups – and there are many – are a good place to find free support.

The World Wide Web (WWW) Part magazine, part art form, part encyclopedia, the World Wide Web is a global hypertext system. (For more information on hypertext, see page 50.) Pages of text and pictures contain highlighted words which link to relevant information stored elsewhere either as part of the same document or part of a different document on another computer in a different country. Although the Web is visually appealing and easy to use, it is also slow (some pages

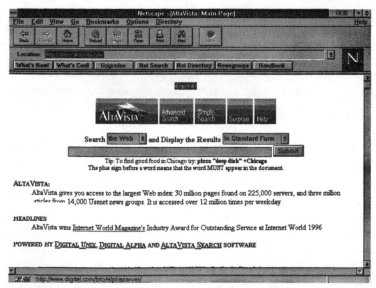

AltaVista is a free on-line indexing service that helps Internet users find information on the World Wide Web

can take minutes to appear on screen), and therefore can be expensive.

The most useful thing the WWW can offer the user is international advertising space. Many organisations and individuals now have their own Web 'pages' and it is an excellent way to reach millions of potential customers.

News wire services These offer direct access to Reuters, Associated Press and other news agencies. A number of electronic newspapers (such as *Clarinet*) are also available. For the most part, the cost of these services is in addition to the normal Internet connection. The advantage of subscribing is that you get the news as soon as it happens. Several news-filtering services, the equivalent of press-cutting agencies, are starting to become available.

Do I need the Internet?

You should seriously consider an Internet connection if:

- you deal regularly with overseas businesses with e-mail contact addresses
- you need access to the latest news and stock-market prices
- you already have a basic level of computer literacy and would like easy access to expert help on a wide range of subjects.

As a means of obtaining computer support, however, the Internet is not a cheap option. Even the cheapest services cost over £100 a year, not including telephone bills, and this in no way guarantees support. If you ask for computer advice in one of the public discussion areas your query may well be read by thousands, perhaps even tens of thousands of users, but it is always possible that none of them will reply or even know the answer.

However, if you are considering an Internet connection for other reasons, such as e-mail, this can be an excellent way to get help. On the whole users do reply to genuine questions. The situation is even better on on-line services such as CompuServe (see example of typical on-line service access software opposite), which give you direct, more formal access to manufacturers' support teams and other users of their hardware and software.

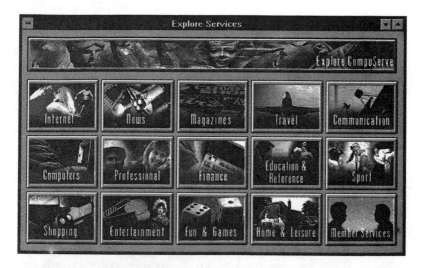

The Internet and children

The unrestricted nature of information on the Internet means that some of it is frank and explicit, and therefore unsuitable for children. Some on-line services, such as America OnLine, include parental control options which mark certain areas 'out of bounds'. For those with more direct access, a number of products have become available which attempt to restrict what children can and cannot find on the Internet, filter out offensive language and optionally keep a list of Internet accesses so that parents have a record to refer to. None of these products is totally foolproof. Although they will deter and protect younger Internet users, many computer-literate teenagers will be able to work around them in short order.

This is one of the most politically difficult areas surrounding Internet access, and a workable solution is still some years away. In the meantime, parents should be aware of the dangers and should look out for reviews of the relevant products in the more home- and family-oriented computer press.

Integrated communications

Fax machines and answering machines are a common sight in small offices. Both of these can be replaced by their computerised versions, saving space and sometimes paper.

Network hardware

All on-line services use a piece of hardware known as a **modem**. Modems connect to the telephone line and allow your computer to send information to any other modem-equipped computer in the world. Most modern modems also include a fax facility. With the right software – which is often included when you buy the modem – you can send a fax directly from your computer without having to print it out on paper first. The computer can easily maintain a 'fax address book' for common destinations and can also send copies of the same fax to many different addresses automatically. Your computer can also receive faxes. These can be viewed on screen, or printed out if you have a printer attached.

Some modems also offer voice recording. With the right software these can be used as an electronic **voice mailbox** service. Outsiders can dial in and leave voice messages for different people on a single telephone line. Their respective mailboxes can be password-protected to make sure only the intended recipients hear their messages.

At the lower end of the market voice-recording technology can be quite crude and the software may not be up to professional standards. But a fully working professional system – which may cost only slightly extra – can boost the image of a small business. For companies that do not have their own switchboards, voice mail can be used as a kind of automatic receptionist. The computer is able to store callers' messages and even to maintain separate password-protected 'mailboxes' for each employee. Voice mail prevents interruptions in meetings and prevents a build-up of stress when calls interfere with important work. It can also save money, as one computer can do the work of a number of answering machines.

The voice-mail system can also be used with pagers. Users can dial in and send a pager message via the computer. The computer can pass the message on to the appropriate pager number.

One problem with fax modems is that they can only transmit information generated by your computer. If you are a designer or artist and need to fax hand-drawn work on a regular basis, or you work with cuttings or other kinds of printed material, you will need to invest in a **scanner**.

A scanner takes an image, be it a sketch or a photograph, and converts it into a form that the computer can use. Once the image has been scanned in, it can be sent as a fax. Some scanners include software for **optical character recognition (OCR)**. This enables the scanner to read printed text and to convert it into text on screen. This can save retyping. Budget scanners tend not to be very reliable, so OCR – even when it comes as a free package – should be treated only as an interesting optional extra. More expensive OCR packages do a much better job and some are used professionally in the publishing trade to scan in copy supplied from faxes and manuscripts for later editing. It is not yet possible to scan in handwritten text so do not expect to get good results from anything other than high-quality printed text and always proof-read the text afterwards. Some fax software includes OCR facilities, so that a fax can be instantly converted into text.

Bulletin boards and on-line mail-order

Some companies offer their own bulletin board service (BBS). This is a public access information and message area that anyone with a modem can dial into. The software for this is very affordable.

You can use the board as a billboard for free advertising and as a way of keeping in closer touch with your clients. Clients can place orders at any hour of the day or night.

If you work far from home and use a portable computer but still need access to your main office system or if you need to share information acquired in the field with colleagues working back at the office it is worth setting up your own BBS. (You can use the Internet to do this, but it is not ideal if you need to work with pictures or diagrams.)

CASE HISTORY: Emma

Emma Summers works as an architect in a busy London practice. She uses the company's bulletin board to help with last-minute changes to presentations.

'*A client will often change his or her mind about an element of the project at the eleventh hour. When that happens I phone the office and colleagues create a new set of drawings or visualisations using their powerful computers, and I upload these to my computer via the phone line in my hotel room. Then I can present these to the client later the same day. We've done this a couple of times now, and it's got us something of a reputation, as well as getting us the contract.*'

CHAPTER 7

JOB-SPECIFIC SOFTWARE AND COMPUTER UTILITIES

ALL THE software we have discussed so far has been aimed at general-purpose business use, but your computer can also help you with your work itself. Job-specific software is not as widely available as the common business-related packages. It is usually written by professional users for other professional users in the same trade. They tend to work independently of the large software manufacturers and often sell their products as **shareware** – a 'try-before-you-buy' system discussed in Chapter 8. Many of these programs are advertised in specific trade journals.

CASE HISTORY: Ted

Ted Smith runs a small electronic design consultancy.

'Computerising some aspects of my trade has freed up a lot of my time. First, we can model circuitry mathematically without having to build it. There are a lot of calculations involved in design, and now the computer does them. So we have time to experiment with different ideas and approaches when attacking a problem. We can also answer "what-if?" questions such as checking for the effect of component tolerances.

'Second, the computer helps with circuit board layouts. This used to be very time-consuming. You have to lay the components out within a certain area and then work out where to make the connections. It's a tough job to do by hand, and there used to be a lot of trial and error involved. There was no guarantee we'd got it right either. The computer does it all for us automatically. It also prints out the track pattern, and

we can use that as the master artwork for the circuit boards. On some projects we've cut development times by 75 per cent.

'I found the software in a shareware catalogue. Off-the-shelf products tend to be expensive. The shareware was much cheaper, and I've been in touch with the author with suggestions that he's included in new versions. If there are any problems I can call him up and ask him about them. Of course not all shareware authors live in the UK, so I've been lucky there. There is also a level of personal contact you wouldn't get with a larger company.'

Software can also be used for non-technical jobs and more and more trades of every kind are taking advantage of the possibilities that computers offer. Whatever kind of work you do there is a good chance you will be able to find software to help you do it more effectively.

CASE HISTORY: Delia

Delia Shepherd breeds toy dogs known as affenpinschers. She uses a computer to keep track of pedigrees and also to watch out for possible genetic defects.

'I used to draw the dogs' family trees by hand, but now I get the computer to do it. They're not just for fun. A very small number of dogs are believed to suffer from a rare recessive gene which can cause them problems. The computer helps me keep track of which dogs are likely to have the defect, and I keep that in mind when arranging matings.

'The software isn't particularly hard to use. It's advertised in the popular dog-breeding magazines and is fairly affordable. I don't know much about computers and I'm not really interested in learning. In fact I don't know how any of it works at all. A friend set it up for me and showed me how to use it.'

Computer-aided design

Some work-specific products are popular and widely available. Although they started out as tools for particular trades, they are now almost as common as the ubiquitous business office suites.

Computer–aided design (CAD) is one of the largest of these practical applications. At its simplest CAD offers an electronic replacement for the drawing board. Plans can be created and printed out without the tedious and time–consuming business of drawing them by hand, and changes can be made on screen without leaving a trail of untidy and distracting correction marks.

An architect, for example, using a CAD system can create perspective drawings from any position and is able to shade materials (the technical word is *render*) in different ways, so that images can seem almost real.

CASE HISTORY: William and Martha

William and Martha Philips, who design and install kitchens, use a CAD program to help with floor layouts and three-dimensional visualisations.

'*We started off with a simple package designed for architects that gave us a top-down or side-on view of the working area. It was like a drawing board, but on the screen. We could draw in different units, experiment with positioning, and then show a client the various possibilities. The greatest advantage was the speed with which we could move things around. If someone said, "No, I want the washing machine there", we could pick it up, move it and shuffle everything around to suit. That's what makes CAD so much better than a drawing board. Once we'd got the layout settled, we'd use that and the side elevations as the basis for the final plans. The computer did these too.*

'*At the moment we're experimenting with a system that enables us to do three-dimensional visualisations of a finished kitchen. The pictures are in colour, and have the right textures – wooden areas appear woody and so on. We can show night and day views by changing how the scene is lit. We can even move around inside a view to try all the different perspectives, including impossible ones such as looking down from the ceiling!*

'*It's very impressive, but it's also very time-consuming; it takes ages to create a new design. We have a library of units – or rather, pictures of units – inside the computer and we can slot these into a view without having to redesign them from scratch. Even then, telling the computer exactly where every last thing has to go can take ages.*

'CAD is very demanding: we have a powerful machine – fast processor, lots of memory, a big screen – and you couldn't do what we do with less. The 2-D stuff is fine on just about any machine, but if you start working in three dimensions you need something that can really move.'

Image manipulation

While CAD is used for plans and diagrams, image-manipulation software works with photographs, illustrations and other images. This is a rapidly growing field, which is now encompassing some of the work previously reserved for professional photographic studios. Some photographers have embraced the technology wholeheartedly; others are still using traditional methods. Image manipulation can be used to help with advertising and promotion.

CASE HISTORY: Lyle

Lyle Kennet used a combination of image manipulation and desktop publishing to produce a brochure and price list for his software sales company.

'We used to use a photographer for the photos, and I'd hire a design shop to do the layout. This year I thought I'd have a go myself. I took the photos at home on the dining-room table – I used a sheet for a backdrop – and had them developed on to CD-ROM. You can get this done in the high street now. It's about £30 for a roll of film and around £10 for the blank CD, which can hold hundreds of snaps. You can keep adding to it, so it's like a photo album on a disk.

'I'm no expert and the photos weren't actually that great, but I ran them through the Adobe Photoshop package to sharpen them up and bring out the colours. I also added some interesting background effects.

'I used a standard DTP package to lay out the photos and text. It took about two days to do the double-page spread. I sent it to the printer on a data cartridge, and we got the price lists back soon after.

'I based the design on what we'd used in the past. The logo was already in the computer, and the rest just slotted in around it. It's not

quite as slick as a designer could do, but it does the job. It took me about four days, doing it in my spare time. I think I saved myself something like £2,000. It will be even quicker next time, and I can re-use some parts when I do it again.'

Route planners

Route planners are automated maps. You specify a start and a destination, and the computer works out the best way between the two points. The possible criteria for 'best' include the fastest, cheapest or shortest route, and the computer can combine all of these to create a preferred route based on your personal preferences, so if you dislike motorway driving then the computer will try to avoid motorway routes. Typical speed and fuel consumption figures are used to give an estimate of journey time and fuel cost.

Route planners have proved invaluable for haulage firms, courier companies and sales forces, as they make it possible to estimate costs and delivery times accurately and to work out the most time- and cost-efficient ways to move people and products around from place to place.

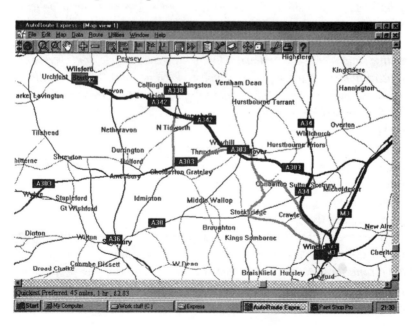

CASE HISTORY: Melanie

Melanie Scott is a sales rep with a major cosmetics company and she uses a route planner to help her manage her time efficiently.

'When I started I used to sit there with a map trying to work out the best way to visit all our customers. Now I get the computer to do it for me, and it does a much better job. On average I think it's saved me between half an hour and an hour a day when I'm on the road. I get less stressed from the driving and I can work out my expenses in advance.'

Project management tools

These are used to keep track of large projects. Project management (PM) consists of planning, communicating and managing, and PM tools help with the first two of these.

CASE HISTORY: John

John Adams runs an architect's practice and has been using a project-management software package for three years.

'The architect's job is not just to design the building so it fits the setting and doesn't fall down. We're also responsible for overseeing construction as a whole. This involves keeping track of information, resources, raw materials and people to make sure the project is finished on time and within budget.

'The most useful PM tool is the Gantt chart, which shows a breakdown of the project in terms of what is due to happen when. With the software we use we can track resource usage as part of each Gantt line, so that we keep abreast of costs. It also shows where we are, as opposed to where we should be. If the project starts to slip, the software warns us, and we can take action.

'We use critical path calculations to work out which parts of the project matter the most. This helps us identify key tasks that we can't afford to have running late. The next stage is to assign the tasks to people and that's when the different charts come in useful. It's a good way to give everyone an overview and to show where they fit in. They can then take

the information away and use it with their own teams. Since using the software we've been a lot more organised about the work that we do, and it's been a great help to the practice.'

Computer utilities

As well as tools to help you with specific jobs there are also more general computer utilities which make your computer work better, faster and more efficiently. They are available to help with most aspects of computer use. If you are a beginner you can usually get by without them, but more confident users find them useful.

Screensavers

These are entertaining, if largely useless, decorative programs which blank out the screen if you stop working on your computer for longer than a set time. On older machines there was the possibility that a picture on the screen could burn into the phosphor if left for too long. Screensavers were developed to prevent this. After a period of inactivity the picture on the screen changes to something with some movement. As soon as the user presses a key or moves the mouse the old screen is restored and work can continue.

Over the years screensavers have developed into something of an art form. A screensaver called 'After Dark' started the trend with a famously surreal scene of flying toasters, complete with wings, and included options such as a fish tank with convincingly animated fish and ferns. This led to increasingly ornate animated cartoon sequences, some with full musical backing, and various film and TV tie-ins.

Unless you enjoy the sheer whimsy of these products and have no objection to spending money on random entertainment, you can ignore most screensavers. Modern monitors are much less prone to burn-in, and newer software such as Windows comes with a simple but effective screensaver of its own. The only good practical reason for using a screensaver is that some offer a measure of security if you need to leave your machine unattended for a time.

Disk doublers

When computers had much less storage space a popular accessory was the disk doubler. By compacting the information into a smaller space this could give you up to twice as much free space using your existing hardware.

However, disk doublers have several disadvantages: very occasionally information would simply be lost; compatibility problems with certain kinds of software were also reported; and speed was another problem, because compacting and restoring information every time the disk is accessed slows work down considerably.

In general, disk-doubler software is not necessary any more for desktop work. Storage hardware is now so cheap that there is no reason to settle for a small disk and augment it artificially, when for a few tens of pounds more you can buy all the storage space you need.

For users of portable computers, however, disk doublers can be a useful option. Storage areas on portables are much smaller, and it is much more expensive to buy larger sizes for a portable than for a desktop. If you have a lot of software installed you could easily find yourself running out of space, and a disk doubler can solve this problem.

Some computers come with free disk-doubling software. All PCs that use the MS-DOS system (most of them, in other words) have an option called Doublespace which is a simple disk doubler. If you need this option you should ask your dealer to set it up for you before you buy the machine.

Extending memory

Apple computer-users can purchase a useful product called RAM Doubler. This works exactly like a disk doubler, except it doubles memory space rather than storage space. RAM Doubler slows the computer down by a few per cent, but otherwise it is a very good way of expanding what your machine is capable of without spending money on real memory. (PC owners who use the Windows operating system have the equivalent of a RAM

Doubler in the form of the **virtual memory manager** that is part of the control panel.)

Memory managers

IBM-compatible PCs use memory in a notoriously inefficient way. The original design for the PC set an upper limit of 640Kbytes on how much memory could be used. At the time it was felt that this would be enough for any user. A few years later, however, it was clear that this was in fact a major limitation of the design.

As a result two different schemes – extended memory and expanded memory – were devised to break through the limit. Neither of these works particularly efficiently and both slow the whole computer down.

A related problem is that some software – especially **software drivers**, which are small programs that control hardware extras such as soundcards and CD-ROM drives – need to use certain sections of memory. When a PC is fitted with a large selection of extras, these sections can become very crowded and there is not enough room for other software. As a result the computer will flash an 'out of memory' error message on the screen, even though there is plenty of free memory inside the machine. Memory managers solve this problem by arranging the drivers so they take up as little room as possible.

All IBM-compatible PCs are now supplied with a free program called MemMaker which offers basic memory management. This program has its limitations and if you have tried it and are still having problems, you will need a commercial memory manager. One such is QEMM from QuarterDeck which is designed to solve memory-related problems. Very occasionally it runs into compatibility problems with some kinds of software but, on the whole, it does the job well.

PCs and software that use the new Windows 95 system are much less prone to these kinds of complications. Windows 95 can – in theory – be set up to make the best possible use of all the available memory whatever the application, and can also run older games with full control over how the memory should be set up for each one. In practice, Window 95 isn't perfect, but it is a huge improvement on the convoluted and confused system that earlier PC users had to contend with.

Uninstallers

Another useful utility is the uninstaller. When you install new software, it copies information to various parts of your machine. Removing this information later can be very time-consuming if done manually.

The best uninstallers keep a list of the type and location of new information added by a software package. You can then uninstall the software with a single command. A less useful type tries to guess where information is kept. These will often ask you first before they delete anything. Unfortunately, even experts can be confused about what is and is not relevant to a given piece of software.

In general if your set up is fairly fixed and you do not spend a lot of time trying out new software, then you will not need to worry about using an uninstaller. If you plan to add to your computer throughout its life, however, then it can be well worth investing in one of these simple and useful tools.

System checkers

Some products claim to offer PC support 'out of the box'. They look at your computer and your applications, check out the whole system, warn you of any problems and sort them out for you automatically.

These can be very appealing to beginners. Unfortunately, in practice few of the current crop work as well as advertised and many are useless. Although they offer help for popular software, this often applies to versions of software that are no longer current. The troubleshooting features are also limited. If you want support you will need to learn how to do it yourself or pay an expert to do it for you.

Compression and decompression software

When archiving or transferring information from one computer to another it can be useful to compact software and data so they take up less space. This is a two-way process. First, compression software is used to perform the compaction. This squeezes the information into a smaller space, but also renders it temporarily unreadable. To restore it to its original form decompression software reverses the process. Shareware (discussed more fully in the next chapter) is often supplied in compressed form, as this is the only way that a complete package can be made to fit on to a single floppy disk. Compression and decompression tools such as PKZip and PKUnzip are the most popular, and both are available as low-cost shareware.

General-purpose 'tool kits'

These include a collection of useful tools such as Norton's Commander to help you manage your computer more efficiently. Many of these have been rendered redundant by the newer operating systems (Windows for the PC, and Mac O/S for Apple machines). If you use an older operating system, however, they can make your machine easier to use – rather like the computer equivalent of a Swiss army knife. A good example of a typical tool they include is the undelete utility, which recovers information if you accidentally delete it. Another useful option is a graphic display of the way that information is arranged on your computer's hard disk. This makes it easier to find what you are looking for and also to copy and move information from one place to another.

CHAPTER **8**

CHOOSING THE RIGHT SOFTWARE

IT IS important to avoid buying software without trying it out first unless you have absolutely no alternative. A 'try before you buy' approach can save time, temper and money in the long run. To a large extent, the software you choose determines whether you will be happy with your computer.

Training courses can be a good way to try out software before buying it (these are discussed in more detail in Chapter 11). Another alternative is to visit a dealer. This can present some problems, however, as many dealers and high-street stores will have neither the time nor the inclination to demonstrate a software package in detail. In itself, this is useful as it can show you which dealers are prepared to be helpful. A dealer who is interested enough to discuss and demonstrate your software options is preferable to someone who resorts to high-pressure sales talk.

Magazine reviews can be another useful guide. Many magazines run multiple tests where different products are compared with each other. Even if you do not understand them fully, you will get some idea of how well one piece of software rates against another. The best reviews include usability and productivity ratings, and use independent testers in work-related situations. These give an excellent indication of how easy it is to use a piece of software, and also how easy it is to get useful work done with it (the two are not always related).

Free offers

Free copies of trial software are often given away with computer magazines. Sometimes the software is fully functional, but not the latest version: a special offer inside the magazine lets you buy the current version at a reduced price. Alternatively, the software is a trial version which is limited in some way; it may be designed to work for a certain number of days, or a set number of times.

Older trial versions are an excellent way to try out software. As software dates far more slowly than hardware, you may find that an old version does everything you want it to. Unfortunately, manuals are not usually supplied with the software, although they may be available for a small charge from the manufacturer. Paying the extra also renders you eligible for free help from the manufacturer.

Limited-use trial versions allow you to try software for nothing. There are no notable drawbacks to this approach, and if you buy the full version it may be possible to keep the work you created using the limited one.

A variation of the trial version is the **encrypted** demonstration. This contains both a demonstration copy of the software that you can try out in the normal way, and a full working version which can be used only with a special access code. To obtain this code you telephone the manufacturers with your credit card details and make a payment, they give you the code over the telephone and agree to send any manuals and other extras you need.

Be wary of this kind of offer. You may be tempted to make an impulse purchase. Test the software *thoroughly* before buying to be sure it really does meet your needs. You will pay the full recommended price for software bought this way, whereas by shopping around you can often get a sizeable discount on software.

Demonstration versions and money-back guarantees

Some business software vendors offer a 'no-quibble, money-back guarantee'. You can try their software for a limited period (usually 30 days) and if you return it you get a full refund. This kind of approach gives you the relaxed opportunity to try out competing products. Always ask if this kind of deal is on offer before you buy software.

Shareware

Shareware (often known slightly inaccurately as **public domain**) software is explicitly provided on a try before you buy basis. The software is available for a nominal amount and comes with a legal agreement which states that it may be used for an evaluation period – typically 30 days – without payment. Once this time has elapsed the software must be either **registered** – you do this by sending a cheque to the author – or removed from your computer.

Most shareware is produced by independent software writers who work from home and do not have access to the development resources of a large company. The quality of such software can vary. The best shareware packages can compete with professional products costing many times the price, and for those on a very tight budget can be a cost-effective alternative to mainstream products. The worst examples are badly designed, hard to use and unreliable. Some professional products are also badly designed, hard to use and unreliable, but they are, as a rule, at least partially usable. Unfortunately this is not always the case with shareware.

Many shareware authors add incentives when users pay for their work. These include copies of a 'full' version of the software with useful extra features, or perhaps a properly printed and bound manual. (Most shareware documentation is supplied as text on a floppy disk.) There may be some kind of irritating regular message or warning that you are using an unregistered copy. Registered versions will not have this.

Some authors take a more extreme approach and release shareware which is all but crippled. For example, an accounts package may allow a maximum of 100 entries, or word-processing software will only work with very small documents. Limitations like these can be irritating, but even a hamstrung version of a package will still give users an idea of whether the package suits their needs.

Many shareware authors are in the United States, and payment is often specified in US dollars. It is rare for an author to accept foreign currency or credit cards. Registration can be made difficult if the address given in the documentation is no longer the author's current address. Some authors have tackled this problem by setting up national dealerships which collect registration fees.

There are two main sources of shareware: bulletin boards (see Appendix VIII); and public shareware libraries. Shareware libraries act as a clearing house for shareware. They do not usually collect registrations but simply keep copies of many different shareware packages which are available for a small fee. The best produce comprehensive catalogues and maintain their own bulletin boards, which allow access to their stock of titles.

Freeware

A handful of software titles are freeware. As the name suggests they can be used by anyone for free. The author maintains the copyright, but the software can be legally copied and used by anyone. (Strictly speaking, only freeware should be called public domain software, as only freeware is genuinely free of copyright charges and hence truly in the public domain. However, the words are traditionally applied to shareware as well.)

Freeware tends to be written by hobbyists or enthusiasts and is unlikely to offer much to the less experienced user. For example, the POVRAY2 computer graphics package can produce very impressive photo-realistic images and animations, but demands a high degree of technical knowledge.

Custom software

Unless your needs are very unusual, you should be able to find a software package off the shelf or a standard package that can be adapted to suit your requirements.

If you cannot find one, you have the option of commissioning a programmer to create some custom software. However, this is not to be undertaken lightly. It is an expensive option: a good programmer can charge in excess of £1,000 a week. It can also be a lengthy option. You may be lucky and come across a programmer who gets the job done in time, but this often proves impossible for any number of reasons, and so it is wise to allow yourself a generous schedule and an equally generous budget.

Software writing is still as much an art as a science, and for many reasons a project can go over time and over budget. It is advisable to negotiate a fixed-rate contract, with an initial payment, a stage payment when the first version is completed and a final payment when everything has been tested thoroughly. The final stage – known as 'bug fixing' – will take the longest. Getting a piece of software 90 per cent right is comparatively easy; getting it 99.9 per cent right sorts out the professionals from the cowboys.

To find a programmer, look in *Yellow Pages* and the classified ads of computer magazines. Your local training and enterprise council (TEC) or business centre may also be able to make suggestions. Follow the same criteria you would use to find a consultant (see Chapter 2). Previous experience is particularly important here. The most appropriate programmer for a project will have done one or more very similar jobs in the recent past and will be able to offer references.

Deciding what you want

Choose your software first and then find the hardware. This rule of thumb bears repetition. It is far more important to choose the right software than the right hardware as most reasonably priced hardware today can handle anything needed to run an office. If you work on this principle you are almost certain to get a smooth-running, efficient system that does what you want it to.

When buying a software package, watch for the following:

Ease of use Does the package do what you want in a simple and straightforward way, or do you have to work around its quirks before you get results?

Features Be wary of packages that claim to do everything. Some office-oriented software packages now come with so many options that a number of the features remain unused. Sometimes a cheap and basic package can be much better value – and prove more useful in everyday terms – than a more upmarket product.

A spreadsheet, for example, is a good general-purpose tool for financial analysis, but if you want something to help with your accounts it may not be the ideal purchase.

Productivity How much more easily and quickly will the software help you get your work done? (This is not quite the same as ease of use.) Some packages are tricky and slow to set up, but once up and running are speedy and efficient. Others are easy to understand, but can seem laboured once you have mastered the basics and are feeling more confident.

The best software includes shortcuts and automation features for commonly repeated tasks. It also has on-line help – a brief summary of the manual within the program itself.

Hardware requirements How much hard disk space does the package take up? How much memory does it need? How fast is it? Here again, modern software packages can be very demanding. A full installation of Microsoft's Office Professional system – a popular package which includes a word processor, spreadsheet, business presentation generator and database – can take up over 60Mb of storage space. Competing packages from other major software companies make comparable demands. If you plan to install a number of applications, you will need to be sure that you can afford the hardware to cope with this.

Operating system requirements Within the hardware specification you will find a reference to an operating system. Operating systems are a special kind of software that run your computer. (For further details on operating systems see Appendix III.)

The last two points are particularly important, as they will dictate what kind of hardware you should buy. Together they give you a detailed hardware specification to shop for.

Software buying tips

When buying software you should be very careful to make sure that it does what you want it to – in practice, as well as in theory. The most widely advertised business packages are **office suites** which include a word processor, a spreadsheet, a database, a business presentation package and also extras such as a personal information manager, or a home accounts program. These may seem appealing at first sight, especially as they are often sold at a discount, but they may not do exactly what you want. If all you want is some simple accounting tools to help with income tax and VAT, and a way of keeping track of your business contacts, you may well get better value from simpler and more specialised software.

CASE HISTORY: Richard

Richard Kent discovered that office suites are not always as useful as they can appear to be.

'I work as a computer and music journalist, and it was becoming obvious that I was losing work because I didn't have a PC. It took me six months of research to find the system I wanted at an affordable price. By then prices had come down as well, which helped.

'I found an office suite package advertised for £175, excluding VAT. This seemed like a very good price, so I phoned the dealer and got him to confirm. He told me it was a "competitive upgrade". I said I didn't even have a PC, never mind any competitive PC software. He told me not to worry – that was all sorted. I gave him my credit cards details and ordered the software.

'It arrived a couple of days later. I installed it, and for a long time was very happy. The word processor was much better than anything I was used to, the computer was very fast, and the organiser was – and still is – a godsend.

'But nine months on, I'm beginning to wonder if I got over-excited. The package also included a business presentation creator, a spreadsheet and a database. I deleted all three of these a couple of weeks after I got the package, and I still haven't used them yet. I may reinstall the spreadsheet to do my tax – but then again, I may not.

'I think these packages are designed for medium-sized businesses and corporate users. They are good packages – there's no doubt about that – but for a single person working at home they're not really necessary. I could have done with more help organising my tax returns and my invoices, neither of which I'm very good at, but they didn't help at all there. I'm sure they could, but I can't be bothered to set them up. And *it would be easier to buy a proper package for exactly those jobs from somewhere else.*

'In general I'd warn people to be cautious of software advertising – especially "free" software. You may be lucky and get exactly what you need, but also you may not. I was lucky in that I got a good deal and didn't really waste any money. If you need a word processor, buy a word processor – and don't get a whole suite unless it's only slightly more expensive, or you know what you are getting, and it really is what you want.'

Upgrade deals

Richard's story illustrates another useful buying tip – the 'upgrade' deal. Some software is quoted with three prices. The first is the official retail price. The second is the 'competitive upgrade' price. This applies if you have a competing software product from another manufacturer; you trade in your old software and get new software in return.

Some dealers will supply you with free software which qualifies for the upgrade deal, so you can buy from them at the reduced rate. The third is the 'version upgrade'. If you already own an older copy of the software, you can get a new copy – with improved features – by paying this price. The numbers and letters after the name of the software are important if you decide on this price level. For example, Word Pro v2.0 means you are buying version 2.0 of the Word Pro program (sometimes the 'v' is left out). The higher the number, the newer the software (thus WordPerfect 6.0 is newer than WordPerfect 5.1). Version numbers are usually included in advertisements. By shopping around you can pick up one of these older versions at a bargain price and use it as the basis for an upgrade deal. Often you will pay less for the old version plus an upgrade than for the new package. You may find that the older version does the job you want and you will not need to upgrade.

Vouchers

With some upgrade deals, however, you may not get the software immediately. Instead, you will be given or sent a voucher which you then pass on to the manufacturer, sometimes with proof of ownership of relevant older or competing software. The software will arrive through the post. This can be irksome if you need to get on with some work quickly. Before ordering an upgrade of any kind, check to see if there are any vouchers involved, and if so, what the time scale will be. If you are going to have to wait for three weeks you may want to reconsider your purchase or factor this delay into your schedule.

Bundles

Another way to get cheap software is to accept a bundle that comes with your computer when you buy it. Many larger hardware dealers include an office suite as a bundle. If you do not want it, you can delete it or choose not to install it, but unless the software is what you want anyway you should be wary of allowing a bundle deal to sway your decision about where to buy.

In practice, some bundles are not quite as good value as they appear.

CASE HISTORY: Ralph

Ralph Harris, a wine and spirits wholesaler, discovered this for himself — but managed not to waste his money.

'I'd been thinking of computerising my operation for a while, and I was asking advice from a friend. After months of checking I'd found a likely-looking deal in a magazine and I wanted to know what he thought. The deal included accounts software for free and a good price for the hardware. There were some other bits and pieces thrown in – a route planner, a couple of games, that kind of thing.

'I was surprised how dismissive he was when I told him about the deal. He told me that most of the software would be pretty useless and that offer deals were put together to shift the software by giving it away.

'All the same, I decided to buy the whole lot. The price was so good that I could add some good software later.

'In fact he was right. The accounts package was terrible, and the games wouldn't even work on my machine. It turned out to have something to do with the way the memory was set up. I phoned the

dealer, and he told me I needed something called a memory manager. As I'm not much bothered about games, I decided to leave it.

'But I must say the route planner has been a great toy and very helpful with deliveries. So it wasn't all completely wasted.'

Disks and manuals

If you do decide that a bundle is right for you, check that the disks and manuals are included.

Having a copy of the software on your hard disk is not enough. If something goes wrong and your hard disk loses the programs you have lost your software. You can of course make safety copies of your own but this can be extremely time-consuming. With manufacturer-supplied master disks this problem can be avoided. The software can be reinstalled and work can continue as before (assuming that your information has also been backed up regularly). The same applies to the manuals. Although modern software often includes a help feature – in other words, help is included within the software itself – this can be sketchy. Access to printed manuals is essential for beginners and for reference.

Most dealers are willing to supply disks and manuals for an extra charge – a typical price might be around £80 for a full set of manuals and disks. Even with this extra cost you may find a bundle can save you money.

CHAPTER 9

CHOOSING THE RIGHT HARDWARE

FROM THE outside one computer looks very much like another. So why are some computers so much more expensive than others? How can you find the one that best meets your needs?

Several factors influence the selling price of a computer. Some, such as performance, can be measured objectively. Others, such as brand image, offer more elusive (some would say illusory) benefits. But to a beginner or a professional user support stands out as being particularly important.

Features to look out for

The following factors will affect the cost of a computer:

Speed A computer's price is directly related to how quickly it can perform a task. Most office work does not require the fastest machines available; an 'average' machine will be sufficient and the best value for money.

Space for your information There is a limit to the amount of information a computer can store. As a rough guide the more your computer costs, the greater the limit. The limit depends on what you want the computer to do. The whole of this book, for example, takes up less than 1/400th of the total storage space available on the computer on which it is being written. Unless you need to keep track of huge amounts of information, have to deal with thousands of clients' records or want to use your computer to work directly with sound or video then the space available in almost any modern machine will fit your needs.

Room to grow Most computers can be upgraded to offer new facilities and better performance. This is easier to do on some machines than on others. Computer technology is improving all the time, and extras designed for the latest machines may not work with older ones.

Deciding whether or not you will need to upgrade can be difficult. Many new features are bought for fun rather than for good business reasons. Fortunately, you should be able to upgrade any modern machine with ease. Older computers are more problematic, and you should assume that you will not be able to upgrade them. (This is something of a simplification as often you will be able to add extras – but not as cheaply or easily as you could with a modern machine. In some cases you may end up spending more than a new machine would cost.)

Build quality Some computers are built more solidly than others. The details are slight and most of them will not be obvious unless you open up the case and look inside. However, these differences can affect long-term reliability and also the ease with which you can upgrade. Buying from a good dealer should ensure that your machine is solid enough for your needs.

Brand image In theory you should get a better-quality product and better support from a large and established manufacturer than a smaller one. But a computer made by a large company with a famous name will cost more than one made by a small-scale start-up business. The reasons for this are partly historical. Larger computer manufacturers traditionally sold to big businesses which could afford to pay higher prices. Over the last few years this has changed, but some of the big-name brands – such as Compaq, Dell and IBM – still carry a price premium. Brand image can be a red herring for the unwary buyer. Unless you are impressed by the products and support service of a big-name manufacturer, there is no good reason to go for the extra expense. A big name does not automatically guarantee you a better computer and may sometimes mean you are paying a lot for some fancy lettering on the case. However, it is more likely that a larger manufacturer will remain in business for the lifetime of the computer. And some of the larger companies, notably Dell and Compaq, do make an effort to provide high-quality support.

Support The important question to ask here is 'What happens if my computer goes wrong?' You might expect the quality of after-sales service to be reflected in the price. This is not always true. Many buyers have found that they get better service from a small, locally based retailer who also sells hardware at a reasonable price. Small companies are sometimes run by enthusiasts who take the time to build up a good working relationship with their customers. A large company will often treat its customers more impersonally.

It is advisable to find out about a dealer's support service *before* a problem occurs rather than after. Although there are no guarantees of support, you can check a dealer's attitude to support by asking a few questions. Someone who is enthusiastic and helpful will give you much better support and in the long term could prove a much better supplier. Good support is vital. It is well worth paying a little extra to be sure of support. Some dealers will take the long-term view and provide you with help and advice in the hope that you will buy from them in the future. Others will take your money and send out the goods, but will not offer any more service. However, if you have access to expert help from elsewhere and therefore do not have to rely fully on the dealer, then you can sometimes get bargains from these latter dealers.

What's inside the box?

By choosing your software first and making a note of the specifications required by that software you are on the way to ensuring that you get a system that will fit your needs.

However, some basic computer knowledge can also be useful. Here is a short introduction to the inside of a computer (more detailed explanations are included in the Appendices).

A computer consists of a main system unit with attached extras such as the keyboard, screen and printer. Inside the main system unit are the parts of the computer that do the actual work. They include:

A motherboard This is the heart of the computer. It holds the processor chip that does the calculations, and also the RAM (random access memory) that the processor uses. The processor does all the work, rather like the engine in a car, and the memory works rather like a desk in an office – it is used as a work area, where information can be held temporarily while being worked on.

Hard disk drive (often shortened to **hard drive**, or **hard disk**) This provides fast-access, longer-term storage and is equivalent to a filing cabinet. Information held in the computer's memory is lost when it is turned off, so it has to be saved to the hard disk beforehand to make sure that it survives. It is loaded from the hard disk when it needs to be used again.

Floppy disk drive This is used to get information into and out of the computer. Software is often supplied as one or more **floppy disks** – small plastic wafers with a metal catch that protects a thin disk of magnetised plastic. The plastic holds the information and the rigid case protects it from finger prints and other hazards.

Memory, hard disk and floppy disk capacities are all measured in **megabytes** (Mb). One megabyte is roughly equivalent to one million letters – including spaces and punctuation marks. You will also come across **kilobyte** (Kb – one-thousandth of a megabyte) and **gigabyte** (Gb – one thousand megabytes, occasionally shortened to 'gig') units of information capacity. The text of this book – which is approximately 70,000 words – takes up roughly 700Kb. A long letter might take up 3Kb. A large piece of software will need around 20Mb. Typical capacities are between 4Mb and 16Mb for a computer's main memory, 1.44Mb for a floppy disk drive, and 500Mb and upwards for a hard disk drive. Floppy disk drive capacities are more or less standard across all machines but the other figures can vary. Hard disk drive capacities are increasing rapidly. By 1997 the standard hard disk size is likely to be at least 1Gb.

Extras are either internal and plug straight into **expansion slots** on the motherboard, or external, plugging into **serial and parallel ports** on the back of the machine. Expansion slots provide a direct connection to the computer's internals and allow you to add extra features, such as sound and graphics, by plugging them straight in. Most computers include blanking plates at the back to hide the slots when not in use.

Serial and parallel ports are connectors on the back of the computer and are used to get information into and out of the machine in a less direct way. The printer is usually connected to the parallel port and the mouse (a small palm-shaped pointing device that is rolled around the desk) is connected to the serial port. (Parallel and serial refer to the way the information flows – either in big chunks or spread out along a single wire.)

Common extras today include:

Soundcard, which allows your computer to record and play back sounds and music. Often a small pair of loudspeakers will come with a soundcard. Less often you will also be supplied with a microphone.

CD-ROM drive, with which, in combination with a soundcard, the computer can play ordinary music CDs. More importantly, it can also access information and software that is now also being supplied on a special kind of CD known as a CD-ROM. Examples include the *Oxford English Dictionary*, some encyclopedias, games and even some business software. CD-ROMs have become popular with manufacturers because they are a good way to supply a lot of information (over 650Mb) on a single small piece of plastic. They are also ideal for the new breed of multimedia applications which combine text, sound and video. It is also possible to have photographs developed directly on to CD-ROMs, so you can load them straight into your computer.

Modem, which is used to transfer information along the telephone line to another computer. Most modems can also send and receive faxes and work as an auto-dialler.

Scanner, which transfers images from paper to your computer. You can take a photograph and scan it across to the computer screen. Once it has been scanned, you can manipulate the images using photo-editing software such as Adobe's Photoshop.

IBM or Apple?

There are two kinds of computer that are widely available and they are sold in slightly different ways. Your choice will depend on the software you want to use. Businesses tend to use the common **IBM-compatible standard** (also known as a PC). Such machines are designed and built by a huge range of manufacturers and are available from all kinds of outlets, ranging from high-street stores to specialist dealers. The word 'compatible' – 'clone' is sometimes used to mean the same thing – means that all these machines are designed to work to the same specification. Hardware and software that work on one modern machine will work on all of them. (Note that this applies only to new designs. Old software will usually work in new machines, but the reverse is not true.) It is easy to exchange information between different brand names and models.

Users with creative or artistic interests tend to favour computers made by Apple. Apple used to control the production and distribution of its machines very strictly. They were made only by Apple itself and sold by a strictly regulated chain of dealerships. This changed in early 1995. Apple is now licensing its technology to a number of other companies and Apple machines are available through many of the same outlets that sell PCs.

In general, Apple machines are much more popular with their users and inspire an almost religious devotion unmatched by other systems. Perhaps this is because Apple-compatible systems – both hardware and software – seem much more colourful and 'human' than their IBM counterparts. Apple hardware also tends to be more appealing aesthetically. However, the IBM market has the advantage of scale. Competition is very fierce within the PC market, and prices can and do fall spectacularly.

For home or light business use there is very little to choose between the two lines. The same kinds of software are widely available on both machines, and it is a case of trying out each brand to see which feels the most comfortable and easy to use.

For more serious and professional use, the markets diverge significantly. Apple machines are used more for applications such as design, and book and magazine publishing. Both the hardware and the software tend to be geared towards these areas of use. IBM machines are used for everything else. Equivalent 'creative' software is available, but powerful IBM machines tend to be used more for business-oriented applications. Prices diverge at this level too, with Apple machines becoming approximately half as expensive again as equivalently powerful IBM models – although this does not become a factor until the very top-line models in each range are compared. Apple machines tend to hold their resale value.

How much can you expect to pay?

Even with the pace of technological development, computer prices have stabilised into price bands, from second-hand 'antique' to showroom-new. (Please note that these are prices for the main hardware only – the main system unit, the keyboard, the screen and an operating system. You will need to allow for software, support, maintenance and other extras such as a printer before you can estimate the total system price.)

Vintage – between £50 and £100

These machines are more or less obsolete and are only available second-hand. They cannot be upgraded to offer new features, they work very slowly and many cannot work with modern software at all. For tasks such as basic word processing, however, they can fit the bill perfectly. Many are still being used successfully ten years after they were purchased.

Dated – between £100 and £250

Although almost obsolete, these machines are still viable for light-duty work such as letter-writing and basic accounts. They are significantly more powerful than vintage machines, but not powerful enough to work with the very latest software. There are severe restrictions on how easily they can be upgraded so they should be bought on a 'what you see is what you get' basis, rather than with an eye to future possibilities. Many of these machines are still used in offices today, although they are now available only on the second-hand market.

Recent – between £250 and £500

These machines are at the trailing edge of recent developments and are still available new. They can be upgraded but there will be limits to what they can do. They will work with the latest software, albeit very slowly. They offer a good deal for medium-duty work such as simple spreadsheets and payroll calculations for a small company.

Because Apple has such a tight grip on its market, Apple computers do not appear in this price bracket. When older models become obsolete Apple simply replaces them with newer and more powerful designs. Only very rarely are these older machines sold off as 'bargains'.

Entry level – between £500 and £750

These are the cheapest of the modern machines. They will work with all the latest software. It is possible, but not certain, that you will be able to upgrade them to work with the very latest extras.

Although much faster and more powerful than older machines, they may appear slow when compared to more expensive models. However, this speed difference will only become apparent when you attempt more demanding work. More modest applications will hardly show any difference at all.

Established – between £750 and £1,000

These offer the best price/performance ratio of any computer design. They provide enough speed and power to cope with recent software and can easily be upgraded. If you expect your needs to increase over the next couple of years, you should consider an established machine.

Advanced – between £1,000 and £2,000

These offer more performance than the established designs and are intended for users who require speed. Typical applications include professional-quality DTP, financial analysis and graphic design.

There is often some overlap between this category and the leading edge, which means that some of these advanced machines may use the latest technology. For reasons given below these should be treated with suspicion. If in doubt, ask your retailer how long a particular design has been available. If it is less than 18 months, you are almost certainly dealing with a leading-edge machine and all the comments below will apply.

Leading edge – between £1,500 and £10,000

These machines are the very best that are available. However, as with software it is a good idea never to buy a completely new design. In the industry the leading edge of technology is sometimes known as the 'bleeding edge' because it can cause users so much heartache. Competition between manufacturers is fierce, and there is a lot of pressure on the industry to keep ahead of the market with new and faster designs. Products are often released before they have been fully tested. If you are using a computer to maintain a business, you cannot afford to be in a position where your computer works only occasionally, gives wrong results or deletes work without notice.

This level of computer is also far too powerful for everyday use. In an everyday office environment most of that power will be wasted. Leading-edge systems are designed for demanding applications such as sound and video editing, architectural visualisation and software development.

Desktop vs portable

You have one more choice to make when deciding on a specification, and that is whether or not to buy a portable computer. The advantages of a portable are obvious – you can use it anywhere, you can keep your important information with you all the time, and you can even use it to keep in touch with a larger computer at home or at the office.

There are disadvantages too: cost and security. Portables tend to be much more expensive than a desktop machine with a similar specification; you can pay £6,000 for a top-of-the-range model. As for ensuring the security of your information, you can install password protection on your portable, but anyone who is computer-literate can work around most password systems fairly quickly.

Battery life and weight are two further considerations. Only the very best portables offer more than a few hours of useful working time, so their range in the field is limited. Some portables are quite heavy: the shirt-pocket computer that can replace a desktop machine has not quite arrived yet.

Some people like the freedom of a portable, and if you can see yourself writing letters in bed before breakfast then a portable will be perfect for you. But for most ordinary office tasks a desktop machine will be cheaper, safer and easier to maintain and to use. (See Appendix VII for more details on portables.)

Obsolete bargains

You will often see computers advertised for less than £500. Many of them are machines that are now obsolete and being sold off as bargains. Depending on what you want from your computer these can offer good value. However, modern machines can be upgraded to make them more powerful and therefore a better investment in the long run, as their effective working life is extended and they can be made to work with more modern and powerful software tools. This will not apply to an obsolete machine. It will be harder to upgrade, will not work with modern software and, eventually, it may even need to be sold or thrown away completely.

However, in practice this may not be a problem. For simple, undemanding tasks a cheap obsolete machine may be perfect, as long as you buy it knowing its limitations. If you cannot envisage your computer needs expanding significantly in the near future, then an older machine can be a good buy. Bear in mind, that if it is very old you should check for the availability of consumables in the same way that you would for a second-hand machine.

Upgrades

All recent computers can be upgraded to take advantage of new technology as it becomes more widely available. If you buy a reasonably priced computer – costing around £1,000 or so – you will almost certainly find you have a range of upgrade options to choose from.

When starting out, however, it is prudent to ignore these until you are familiar with your machine and have got the most you can out of it. If you have an older machine you may find yourself under pressure from trade magazines (perhaps from even friends) to bring it up to more modern standards. Think long and hard before you do. If your computer serves all your current needs, there is no reason for you to upgrade. You should only start to think about this seriously if you feel that your machine is annoyingly sluggish at times, or if some new software arrives which could be useful to you but will not work on your machine.

Deciding whether to buy a high-specification model or a low-specification one that can be upgraded later can be a bit like playing the futures market on the Stock Exchange. In general, it can be worth buying a slightly more powerful machine than you need. For office work, however, it is unlikely that a working system will need to be updated more than once every few years at most. This corresponds to the time it takes a generation of computers to move down from the leading edge to obsolescence. It also corresponds to the four-year writing-down period for capital tax allowances. It is not usually advantageous to get a cheap machine with a view to upgrading later.

The situation is slightly different for home computers that are used for playing games as well as for work. Surprisingly, perhaps, games are much more demanding of computer power than most office applications. You will find that a computer used for games has a much shorter active life and will also need to be upgraded regularly. If games are a serious interest then consider buying the very best computer you can afford.

Buying step by step

By choosing your software first, you have already decided on the hardware to make it work. Most software comes with a minimum, or a typical, hardware specification which is mentioned somewhere on the packaging or in the manual. You can quote this directly to a dealer, even if you do not understand what the words mean. Where possible, choose a 'typical' or 'recommended' rather than a 'minimum' specification, as these will give you the extra power to work comfortably. By following the specifications you will get a computer that does what you want, rather than one the industry wants to sell you. What you choose depends on your requirements. If you foresee your needs expanding, choose a better and more powerful machine than the software specification suggests. If you are looking for a system for basic office work that you can install and forget ignore the high-pressure sales techniques and follow the specifications.

Once you have a rough specification, you can start contacting a few dealers. The best place to look first is in your local *Yellow Pages*. Quote the specification you need, explain which software you will be using, mention that you are a beginner and will need good support, and see what kind of response you get. If you find someone sympathetic and helpful, ask if they can do a package deal which includes all the software you want.

In any conversation with a dealer, note down the time and date, the name of the person to whom you spoke, and any prices you are quoted. You can leave any further details, such as warranties and extras, for a later call. Make a list of the dealers who seem knowledgeable and approachable, together with their best quoted prices. If you find a dealer who responds positively on the telephone, it is worth making a visit to see how you are treated in person. Do not be surprised if you find yourself in a shoddy-looking shop instead of a stylish showroom; it is the level of enthusiasm, interest and professionalism which is important.

Your next step is to repeat the exercise with dealers from further afield. You will find these advertised in any computer magazine. Buying long-distance has its drawbacks, but finding out the going rate for hardware on a nationwide basis can sometimes give you a good negotiating position with your local dealer.

The advantage of buying from a larger company – such as Dell or Gateway – is that they are more likely to be financially stable and less likely to disappear overnight. The disadvantage is that they will often charge you more for their services.

Smaller dealers will usually offer slightly better prices. Some machines are assembled in garages and bedrooms, advertised in the low-cost trade weeklies and sold by mail-order. Others are built by huge companies with multi-million-pound turnover. Both kinds of dealer use the same sets of parts, which are bought in bulk from wholesale electronic design companies in South-East Asia. The only thing that distinguishes these wares is the level of support the dealers can offer you, and the care and attention the manufacturers give to assembling their machines.

Advertising ploys

Smaller dealers sometimes quote rock-bottom prices and it is not until you read the small print that you discover that the system is incomplete – a keyboard, screen and mouse are extra. Another tactic is to sell the operating system (DOS, and/or Windows) as an 'optional' extra. This can add around £70 to the quoted price. To get around this you should ask if the price you have been quoted includes everything you need to run your software right away. Then, just to be sure, check if there are any 'extras' you need. As usual you should make a note of the replies.

Another marketing tactic is to pepper a specification with emotive words such as 'fast', 'powerful' and 'huge'. Often such words are used to confuse the unwary and hide the fact that the system is no better – and sometimes significantly worse – than average. The more of these words you find within a specification list, the less likely it is that you are dealing with someone you can trust.

Your shortlist

By now you should have a shortlist of dealers. You still need to sort out support, maintenance and (perhaps) insurance for your purchase and you will also need to think about security and protecting your information. These will be discussed in the following chapters.

CHAPTER 10

INSURING AND PROTECTING YOUR COMPUTER

BEFORE YOU buy your computer, you need to be sure that you are protected from the various things that can go wrong. Computers can and do break down. They can also be stolen or damaged. Sometimes the problems are easy to fix and no harm is done apart from a few hours' delay. At other times the results can be catastrophic, with months or even years of work obliterated in seconds. How can you protect yourself? And what other dangers do you need to take into account?

Warranties

As a first step, it is essential to make sure you get a warranty with your computer. The simplest is the **back to base warranty**. Under this scheme your computer will be repaired, and defective parts will be replaced if, and only if, you send the computer back to the retailer. You pay the cost of this initial delivery, although the retailer usually pays for the return of your machine.

This is the standard minimum warranty you will be offered. It has very serious limitations if you are planning to rely on your machine for business purposes. First, the warranty is worth nothing unless you can return the machine to where you bought it. If your retailer is not local you can expect to pay between £10 and £15 for a next-day delivery using a courier service.

Second and far more important, this kind of warranty does not usually guarantee how quickly your machine will be repaired. If it needs to be sent back to the manufacturer it may take weeks.

If you rely on your computer on a daily basis this kind of delay can be extremely inconvenient.

Reputable dealers may be willing to provide you with a temporary machine while the repairs are being done. This is a useful option to have, but bear in mind that when your computer goes back to the manufacturer, so does all the information – including the software – you keep on it. Even if you keep safety copies of your work, recreating your working environment on a new machine can take anything from an evening to a few days.

A variation on the back to base warranty is known as **collect and return**. Although popular once, it is now becoming increasingly rare. With this warranty you do not have to pay carriage costs. This is a slightly better option, but all the same caveats apply.

Far more useful is the **on-site warranty**. Under this scheme your supplier contracts to send an engineer to you when something goes wrong. Unfortunately, it is still no guarantee that your computer will be repaired immediately.

On-site warranties vary greatly. Sometimes they are available as an optional extra when you buy a machine. You may even get one year's free on-site service as part of the initial purchase deal, and another year or two for an extra fee. However the deal is arranged, it is advisable to check the small print of the service contract. Watch out for the following:

Call-out time A warranty that guarantees that your computer will be looked at within eight hours of your call is worth much more to you than one that states that it will be repaired within five working days.

Charges What exactly does the warranty cover – parts, labour, both or neither? Is there any kind of excess charge for the first part of any costs?

Company reputation Many dealers subcontract their warranties to independent support firms, some of whom are reliable and professional, others are cowboys. Try to get the telephone number of the support company from your dealer. Then telephone the support company and ask about their charges, call-out times and references from customers. The quality, tone and efficiency of the answers will indicate the kind of support you can expect. If you like the way the company works, take the opportunity to ask about their services. You may even want to think about taking out a longer-term contract.

Company stability The worst possible situation to find yourself in is with a warranty contract from a company that has gone out of business. This does happen and the results vary from the inconvenient to the disastrous. You could ask the company directly about its financial stability. Someone in a professional and stable company will understand the need for your question and should be able to reassure you immediately.

Experience and references Does the company know what it is doing? Some firms have been known to claim to maintain certain types of computer, when in fact they have no experience of them at all. If in doubt, ask for references. Experienced and professional companies will be able to provide you with references.

Resources Ask about the company's 'back-room' technical resources and repair facilities. Does it subcontract the work?

Contract Is it possible to see a standard contract in advance? If not – be very wary.

Location The company should be within easy travelling distance or have a local office.

Quality control Is the company certified as complying with the ISO 9000 or older BS5750 quality-control standards? Or is it applying for certification? These impressive-sounding titles guarantee the existence of quality-control procedures, but offer no further assurance that work really is done to high standards. In practice, the certification system seems to be open to potential abuse, and some quality-control professionals are unhappy with the loopholes that exist. It is likely that these standards will be changed soon. In the meantime it is wiser to judge a company's reliability on the other criteria mentioned here.

Insurance

An increasingly popular option for some businesses is to take out insurance. This pays for the cost of any repairs and may also help indemnify your business against problems caused by the loss of your computer.

Getting insurance for a computer used at home can be problematic. If you run an office from home, insurers are likely to consider your computer a business asset and will be unwilling to insure it under a normal home and contents policy. Some companies will insure you, but only if you meet certain conditions – for example, if you receive very few business visitors.

Special home office policies are available. Some of these provide you with the equivalent of a maintenance contract – some insurance policies compare favourably with maintenance arrangements, and you should investigate both to give yourself the widest range of options. Others are fully comprehensive policies which cover you against damage by water, fire, theft, and may even include extra funds which allow you to hire a machine while your original computer is being repaired. A number of policies also include options which cover the costs of 're-instating' data, which can mean recompiling it from the original sources, or paying someone else to do this for you.

Some will even cover you for 'consequential loss', although this is usually an expensive option. This means that if you lose work because your computer is out of action, you will be reimbursed for some or all of your financial losses.

As with any insurance policy, it is a good idea to read the small print to see what conditions you have to fulfil for the policy to be valid. You will normally be charged an excess – typically £50 – if you make any claim. Some policies also stipulate certain security arrangements you need to take to minimise your risks. These vary from making sure that data is safe, by keeping safety copies and checking for viruses, to making your premises as theft-proof as possible – perhaps bolting your computer to your desk. If you work in an 'unsafe' environment, expect to pay extra. Most British policies cover the use of notebook computers in the UK, but if you travel abroad a lot you will usually be asked to pay extra.

Backups

Even without insurance, you can take steps to make sure that your information is as safe as possible. This is *vital*, especially for business use. Your first step is to *save your work regularly* on the computer's hard disk. If something happens it will still be there when you turn on the machine again. Some software has an **auto-save feature** which does this automatically.

Once your information is on disk, you need to make copies and keep them somewhere safe. These are known as backups, and are a time-consuming but essential chore.

CASE HISTORY: Simon

Simon Jones is a computer consultant.

'Half of the phone calls I get are from people who have accidentally lost some work on their computer and want me to try to get it back for them. I try, sometimes I succeed, but often I don't. The users may have deleted what they want by mistake, had a faulty hard disk or had their machine stolen. In all these cases their most urgent need is for the data which is now unavailable for whatever reason. If they had taken regular backups this problem would simply not exist.

'I try to drum into them the value of taking regular backups of work. It may seem time-consuming and silly at the time but it will save heartache and bad temper in the long run.'

Floppy disks are ideal for low-volume work. You can simply copy the information from the computer to a floppy disk. 50Mb is about the maximum you can comfortably archive on floppy disks. (This is how the backup copies of this book were maintained – the text fits on to a single 1.44Mb high-density disk.) Most computers come with a free backup utility that packs the information more tightly on to each disk and also automates the process across multiple disks. As a rough guide, you can expect to spend about 20 minutes archiving 50Mb of information.

For higher volume work, the cheapest option are **QIC (quarter-inch-cartridge) tape streamers**. These use small tape cassettes to store large amounts of information – 250Mb, 400Mb and 750Mb are typical sizes. The units are fairly cheap – around about £200 for a 750Mb system. They are slow, but unlike a floppy disk-based system you can leave them running overnight unattended. The cartridges themselves are also cheap – around £11 for a 250Mb cartridge.

Tape cartridges do not have a reputation for reliability. Where possible you should verify information after you have backed it up to confirm that it has been recorded accurately. Backup software is usually supplied with the tape streamer. You should make sure that it includes a 'verify' option.

DAT (digital audio tape) systems are more reliable, but also much more expensive. At the time of writing DAT systems cost around £700, and offer 2Gb of storage – ample for most situations. The system also uses tape cartridges, but these are much smaller – around half the size of an audio cassette – and much more robust. A DAT system is recommended if you need a 'bullet-proof' backup system.

Tape-based systems suffer from the disadvantage of being linear – the information is arranged in order along the tape. If you want to restore some information that is at the end of the tape, you have to wait for the tape to wind to the right position. A tape system is recommended if you do full backups of everything on a regular basis, which you should do at least once a month, ideally once a week. It is also possible to do incremental backups. These only backup the information that has changed since the last full backup. This should be done daily.

Tape backup systems also suffer from more subtle drawbacks. Tape wear can be a problem if you use the system regularly, and this can lead to wasted time if you regularly have to back up the backups to prevent information loss. Another problem is print-through – information tends to leach to adjacent loops of tape when the tape is tightly wound. In large organisations which maintain huge tape archives, these are regularly unwound and retensioned to minimise this problem.

Magneto-Optical (MO) disks offer a solution to these problems. They work like CD-ROMs except that you can save information to them. Because the medium is circular rather than linear, information can be found much more quickly. MO disks are also very robust. Information can be retained safely for around 40 years on a disk stored at room temperature. The MO system is also immune to interference from external magnetic fields, so disks can be sent safely through the post.

MO disk systems are still quite expensive and capacities are low. A typical system stores 230Mb of information on a 3.5-inch diskette. At the time of writing prices are around £600, and disk blanks cost around £30. Larger systems of around 1.3Gb are also available at about £1,500. Although the MO system is popular for some applications and a number of companies have found that it suits their needs, it is too early to tell if it will become an industry standard.

One final backup option is CD-R — you create a CD with your own information written on it. These special writable CDs are as reliable and robust as any other CD and offer a high capacity — around 650Mb. Disk blanks cost around £10 — much less in bulk. At around £1,500 this is currently the most expensive option, but prices are likely to fall sharply over the next few years. In fact by the end of the century it is likely that this will be the backup standard — and perhaps even the information exchange standard — used on most machines.

Other systems

A number of new products became available during 1995. These are very affordable and work very much like floppy disks, but have greater storage capacities. The most popular are the Iomega Zip and Jaz drives and the Syquest EZ drive range. These are discussed in more detail in Appendix II.

Software backups

As well as keeping your information safe, it is a very good idea to make safety copies of the software you use. If supplied on floppy disks, you should make copies and never use the originals. You will need between 50 and 100 floppy disks to make a backup of a typical full set of business software. Although it is a tedious chore, the advantages of this single task outweigh the disadvantages. If your hard disk loses its information and your software originals have become defective, you will have to buy the software again – even if it is one disk out of ten that is at fault. Making safety copies can save you time and temper later.

Storing backups

All backup copies should be stored somewhere safe and secure. The ideal is a fire-proof safe, or perhaps, if the information is sensitive as well as valuable – a bank safety-deposit box. A cheaper option is simply to keep safety copies somewhere off the premises – perhaps at home, or at a friend's or relative's house. If your business is burgled or burns down, your safety copies are intact.

As a further aid to security you may want to encrypt your work before you back it up. This will make your information look like gibberish – even to the trained eye – and can give you near-perfect security. The most secure encryption software available today is a shareware package called PGP (see page 86). PGP is available from most shareware libraries. It is slightly awkward to use, but provides near-perfect security.

Uninterruptible power supplies

While the UK National Grid is usually solid and reliable, under extreme conditions, or in remote rural areas, the power supply to your computer can become erratic and this can cause problems. In extreme cases a lightning strike or other power surge can actually damage your hardware.

A UPS (Uninterruptible Power Supply) solves these problems. It smoothes out fluctuations in the mains power level so that your computer always receives clean, steady power. UPS units also offer a short-term backup power source. In the event of a power cut your computer will remain on for a few minutes; this will allow you to shut down the system in a controlled way without losing any work.

Although UPS are not cheap – prices range from a couple of hundred pounds to thousands for 'industrial-strength' models – they are recommended if you use your computer for 'mission critical' applications.

If you use a modem, another useful extra is the **line surge protector**. Every year a handful of computers are frazzled by lightning strikes coming in directly over a telephone line. (The risk may seem negligible, but one insurance company reported over 20 lightning-based claims a year.) BT wall sockets include basic surge protection but are not designed to cope with a direct strike. Fitting a surge protector can ensure that your computer stands a good chance of surviving a strike.

Chip coolers

A very useful – and recommended – hardware protection device is the **chip cooler**. This is a small metal radiator (known as a **heat sink**) that clips on to the computer's main processor chip and conducts heat away before it can do any damage. Chip coolers can prolong the life of a chip dramatically by preventing thermal stresses caused as the chip heats up and cools downs. Most examples include a fan that clips on top of the heat sink to make sure that the chip runs cool. (Only fast IBM-compatible processors – the 486 and Pentium series chips – need chip coolers. Older models and all Apple machines work perfectly well without them.)

Viruses

Computer viruses are simple programs that hide among useful information and then copy themselves into your computer. Once there, they copy themselves on to any disks you use. If you swap information with a colleague's machine then that computer will also become 'infected'. Software received over the telephone can also pass on the virus.

Some viruses are harmless, others are irritating and little more than elaborate practical jokes. A handful are devastating and can wipe out all the information inside your machine. Without special tools it is impossible to check whether or not your computer is infected or to do anything about it. Fortunately these tools are readily available, easy to use and affordable.

It is possible to protect yourself from viruses by following a few simple rules. Never swap information with anyone unless you have to. When exchanging information electronically, only software can infect your machine. Text, graphics, sound clips and electronic mail messages are all virus-free. If you transfer any software over the telephone, check for viruses before using it.

If you need to work with other people's floppy disks, **anti-virus software** is recommended. This removes existing viruses and keeps new viruses out of your machine. Anti-virus packages respond only to viruses that have already been isolated and analysed. New viruses are being created all the time. Many packages now include a subscription option that will keep you safe from the latest examples.

Computer security systems

If you work with other people, you may need to make sure that your private information remains private. Short of encrypting information (for example, using the PGP system mentioned above), there is very little you can do to prevent a computer expert from gaining access to your computer. Desktop computers simply are not secure, and most security systems have loopholes.

On PCs, the most secure option you have is to use a **BIOS password** which you type in when the machine is starting up. This can only be changed by opening the case and short-circuiting or removing the battery on the main computer board. There is no easier way to change it if you forget it. Unfortunately not all PCs have this option. Check with your dealer if security is important to you.

For less secure applications, you can use a **screensaver password**. Most screensavers include a password feature which locks your machine so it cannot be accessed if you leave your desk. (A BIOS password offers protection only while the machine is starting up. Once it is running there is nothing to prevent anyone getting access to your records.) Password protection is perhaps the most useful feature of a screensaver. The protection can easily be 'hacked' by an expert, but it will deter casual users from trying to access your machine.

Many networks include reliable security features, most of which are password-based. If you forget your password, your network supervisor will be able to create a new one for you.

All password systems can be fallible if the password is obvious, or obviously visible. Never use a password that can be guessed easily such as the names of friends, children or spouses, or words associated with your hobbies. PIN numbers are another bad choice. The best passwords are nonsense combinations of words and letters which are all but unguessable.

Avoid typing in your password if anyone is standing close by. Never write a password down, but if you have to, don't keep it anywhere near the computer itself. It is traditional in some businesses to keep passwords on sticky notes under the desk or in a drawer or as a note in an address book. Avoid all of these options. Finally, change your password regularly – at least once a month, preferably once a week, perhaps even once a day if security is very important to you.

Some security systems are hardware-based. The most common of these is the **floppy disk lock**, a disk-sized square of plastic that can be locked into the floppy disk slot with a key. Disk locks are a good way to avoid viruses and unauthorised copying of software, but they will not protect you against unauthorised access to your computer.

Computer theft

CASE HISTORY: Josh

Josh Brown is director of a desktop publishing bureau. He has been a victim of computer crime several times.

'It started in 1990. We got in one morning and all our Macs had gone – over £75,000 worth of equipment vanished overnight. It was a complete and utter disaster. The thieves took all our backup systems as well as the main machines. Most people had left backup cartridges in their drives, so we lost the lot.

'That almost killed the business. We lost a lot of work, a lot of goodwill, and it took a long time before our insurers came up with a cheque. Fortunately, we were covered for consequential losses. Otherwise that would have been it.

'We took advice from our insurers when we replaced the machines. As a result we put stronger locks on the doors and fitted an alarm system.

But these gangs are professional, and three months later we were hit again. They broke in through the first-floor windows, ignored the alarm and took everything again. However, by then we were keeping backups and had taken to leaving them somewhere safe each night.

'Now we have bars on the windows, all the locks and the doors have been specially strengthened, and our Macs have been bolted to the desks with lock-down plates. I looked at having the desks reinforced as well, but it turned out to be too expensive.

'We've had no problems since, but it's been a complete pain to live with. Maintenance takes forever now, as we have to pull the machines apart on the spot before we can take them anywhere. And of course you can't just pick up a computer and move it now. You have to unbolt it first. Everyone hates it, and I don't blame them. But it's either that or the risk of losing everything all over again.'

Preventive measures

A senior crime prevention officer with first-hand experience of computer crime advises on how to prevent it.

'I'd look for a good standard of security generally. The first step is to keep the burglars out. That means curtains and blinds to hide the equipment so it can't be seen from outside, as well as good locks.

'Internal security is important. Who's doing the cleaning, for example. If it's contracted out, who are the contractors using? Are they secure, or are they likely to leave the key with someone? Laptops are another problem. Some thieves just walk in in broad daylight and help themselves to anything that isn't watched or secured.

'Once the burglar is in the building the alarm system means he needs to work fast. We [the police] can get to an alarm in under ten minutes, but it's important that the keyholder is on hand to let us in – sometimes this can take an hour or more, by which time it's too late to do anything. If the criminals can get in without an alarm, they'll spend all night taking things apart. Now that lock-down plates are common, some gangs are taking computers apart and just stealing the chips.

'Property marking is another useful deterrent. It makes it harder to resell things. Big organisations such as health and education authorities are going down the route of overtly marking everything very clearly. It's easy to change the case on a PC so it's not so important there, but with Macs it's harder and marking is more of a deterrent.

'For software and work, backups are essential. I've known some businesses that folded when they lost everything because they didn't protect their work. Boxed sets with the original packaging are very appealing to thieves. They can be sold at car boot sales, so I'd suggest people take the software out of the nice boxes and throw them away.

'If you take serial and model numbers, get rid of attractive packaging, anchor the hardware, reinforce the doors, put in an alarm and make regular backups you're as safe as you can be. But we still like to go to individual premises, so I'd suggest people call in their crime prevention officer – the advice is free – preferably before it happens.'

Many insurance companies will ask you to improve security before they will agree to give you a policy. They will consider loss-of-earnings policies for home and business users, but may start to insist you secure your premises. The theft losses have been quite staggering. Some insurers used to do a flat rate, but now are including location-based payments. Premiums can vary by as much as 400 per cent between safe and high-risk areas.

CHAPTER 11

BUYING A COMPUTER – THE SMALL PRINT

THE BULK of the cost of your computer system will come from your initial investment in hardware and software. By telephoning around and asking for quotes you should already have an idea of what these are likely to be, but there are other costs you also need to consider. The most important ones are:

Electricity How much power will your computer draw? Exact figures depend on the make and model involved, but typically you can expect the following:

Computer unit	200W
Monitor	80W
Laser printer	70W
Total	350W

This is roughly equivalent to keeping six 60W lightbulbs lit. A rough calculation shows that this adds between £10 and £15 a quarter to your bill, assuming an average use of around six hours a day.

Consumables If you are considering a laser printer, make sure you find out how many pages it prints before it needs new supplies. Then estimate how many pages you are likely to print. To get a realistic idea of how many you will print, double this number – at least. This allows for mistakes and misprints. Also check consumable costs. Although ink-jet printers are cheaper, if you are printing in bulk the laser is typically one-third the cost of the ink-jet (comparing ink with toner). (See Appendix II for more details on printers.)

You will also need to budget for floppy disks to keep safety copies of your work and your software. Floppy disks can be expensive. It is cheaper to buy in bulk (100 or more) direct from specialist dealers, many of whom advertise in computer magazines. Buying disks in twos and threes from high-street computer, stationery and business stores is not cost-effective. For small quantities the high-street discount chains, such as Argos, offer a much better deal. Buying by the hundred may seem excessive, but it is easy to use this many by keeping regular backups. If you have arranged to make regular backups using some other medium, allow for these in your final budget.

Maintenance, training and support costs How much is your maintenance cover going to cost? How much do you expect to pay for support? At the very least, you should allow for the purchase of books and magazines to help you get the best from your investment. At the other end of the scale you may opt for access to a full technical support line and a few training courses. These costs should be included in your budget before you buy.

Insurance Are you going to insure your machine? Will your policy cover you for a replacement if it is damaged or stolen, or will you also insure yourself against loss of business if your computer becomes unavailable for any reason? You need to decide on just how vital your computer will be to your business, and how much you can afford to be without it – as well as how much you can afford to pay to cover yourself against this.

VAT and delivery charges The prices of most computer equipment are quoted without VAT, so allow for this in your cash flow if you are VAT-registered, or simply write off the extra if you are not. You will probably also have to pay for the delivery of your system. This can add another £20 to the quoted price.

Telephone charges If you are buying any on-line services, allow for their charges, and also for increased telephone-line use. Bills of over £100 a month are not unheard of but can usually be avoided with careful planning.

First, if most of your calls are long-distance, investigate switching to Mercury. Mercury services are significantly cheaper than BT, and you can take advantage of various business deals and 'frequently called number' schemes to cut your costs even more.

Second, try to use the service during off-peak hours. It is possible to set up a system where the computer sends and receives mail and picks up news automatically during the early hours of the morning. Unless you need access to mail immediately, it's worth waiting till after the 6pm watershed.

And third, if you are expecting to spend a lot of time on-line, make sure you get the fastest modem you can. This can halve your costs and is well worth the small extra initial outlay.

Do not underestimate the cost of consumables and other extras.

CASE HISTORY: Colin

Colin Taylor runs a poster and card shop. He tried to expand his business to offer desktop publishing and design services.

'*Doing the work was the easy part. We were getting plenty of casual trade from local businesses. The problem was, it was costing much more to run than I thought. After about six months it became obvious just how expensive our laser printer was. For starters we were getting through reams and reams of paper. What you get on the screen always looks slightly different when printed out. Some clients were very fussy, and it was taking ten or twelve printouts before they were happy.*

'*But it was the other costs that really surprised me. We were getting through a toner cartridge – at £100 a time – every few months. And after a year the drum needed replacing. I worked out that after two years we'd paid out more for the extras than the printer itself. Another big expense was backups. Desktop publishing needs lots of space, and a cheap backup system wasn't enough. We invested in an external tape drive and started to run a proper backup and archiving system. It's worth it for the business because customers can come back to us for minor changes. We can put a new date on a poster without starting from scratch.*

'*And then there's security. We're insured against theft, and that's not cheap. We can't afford a loss-of-business policy – they're just too expensive – so we're only insured on the basis of like-for-like. If we lose the machines, we get new ones.*

'By the time you add it all up, we're spending well over £1,000 a year on extras. If I was starting again I'd look more closely at the price of extras before committing myself. With printers in particular it's worth finding out how much the consumables cost and how many pages they're good for.'

Renting or buying?

You have three options:

- an outright purchase
- purchasing with a loan or other finance
- renting.

Each of these options will affect your cash flow and tax position in different ways.

Buying a computer can represent a sizeable investment for a small business and buying one outright can jeopardise cash flow. However, you can claim this money back against tax as a 'writing-down allowance'. Currently this means the cost is spread over four years. After four years your computer is assumed to be worth nothing (unless you sell it) and you have claimed your initial outlay back against tax.

Computers can also be classified as 'short-life goods' with a separate writing-down allowance. If you sell your computer, you are allowed to offset the loss against tax instead of being taxed on the income from the sale. Because computer equipment depreciates so quickly this can make a significant difference to your tax liability, to the extent where the sale of an obsolete computer at nominal cost can sometimes be very worthwhile indeed.

Purchasing with finance can be a better deal, at least as far as short-term cash flow goes. You will usually need to put up some of the money yourself – banks and loan companies are not keen on 100 per cent loans, unless you are borrowing a lot less than you can afford – but you will be able to spread the cost over a much longer period. If the computer brings in extra work and improved profits, this can be an excellent investment.

Interest payments are also tax-deductible, so in effect you have the loan 'for free'. The capital value of the computer is depreciated in the usual way, and on top of this you simply add the interest from any payments you are making.

Renting is similar, with one important difference. *All* payments are immediately deductible as a direct business expense. Many renting schemes provide the option of buying the machine outright at the end of a set period – usually three or four years. The sums charged are nominal and at the end of the rental period it is highly possible that the computer is still adequate for your needs. An outright purchase can be a sensible option at this point. Rental payments have been written off against tax, so with a single modest payment you can purchase the computer. This final payment can also be claimed as a capital allowance.

One disadvantage of renting is that it can be much more expensive. It is advisable to avoid short-term rentals unless you need the equipment desperately. Most business rental schemes work out significantly more expensive than an equivalent loan repayment system. However, the rental scheme covers you against equipment failure and other problems, and when you include these extra factors in the equation a renting deal can become more appealing.

As ever, you should read the small print in the rental contract to check the nature of the support that is offered. If it meets your needs and is still cheaper than an equivalent outright purchase then renting is more advantageous for you than buying.

Most computer magazines carry advertisements for rental computers. Several high-street stores operate rental schemes. Radio Rentals, working with Olivetti, has a rental scheme for home users which offers good machines, with software, at reasonable prices.

While renting hardware may be a good idea, renting software usually is not. Over the course of a few years you may end up paying two or three times more to rent software than to buy it outright. Some package deals include software at a good price, and some companies ask for extra payment for software. In the latter case, it is worth shopping around to compare the price of buying the software.

Painless buying in detail

Now is the time to talk to each retailer in turn and check the other services they offer, particularly technical support, warranties, money-back guarantees, delivery charges and delivery times. Confirm the quoted price. Make sure you get a price that includes VAT.

If you are buying everything, including the software and a printer, from one supplier it can be worth trying to negotiate a lower price for the package. If the retailer is local and you can collect the goods in person, it can also be worth negotiating a price for cash. Some retailers, especially the smaller ones, prefer to take cash as it avoids cheque charges.

Don't be afraid to haggle! If your retailer refuses to reduce the price, try asking for essential extras (such as a couple of packets of floppy disks or a printer cable) to be thrown in for free. These are often low-margin items for retailers and they can comfortably afford to give them away in small quantities. At worst you will get a refusal. At best you can save yourself some money.

Smaller retailers may well ask you what the best price you heard elsewhere was. Some would rather have your business, even with wafer-thin margins, than lose your custom to a competitor. It is important to be honest here, because if you quote an unrealistic price the next question will often be '...And did they say they had them in stock and ready to go?'

Be wary of high-pressure 'special offer' deals. Some larger retailers will attempt to use sale techniques to close a sale, by implying that the offer will only be available for a limited period. Although very, very occasionally you may miss a genuine bargain, the general trend in the computer trade is for more power at a lower price – even six months can make a big difference. Unless you really want to order right away and have already decided on a particular retailer, then it is prudent to deflect the deliberate salesmanship and simply say that you will think about it.

If you are a complete beginner, ask whether you will be sent any instructions on how to connect up your system before you place an order. A typical PC comes with five or six different items that need to be linked together, and it is not always obvious how this should be done. More thoughtful dealers include an instruction sheet or will be happy to talk you through the process over the phone. Remember to ask about this before you commit yourself to buying, as this kind of small extra can save you a lot of time later.

Confirm your order in writing, either through the post or by faxing it. For those buying by mail-order many magazines offer pre-printed order forms that you can cut out and fill in, and then send or fax to your retailer as appropriate. *It is important to keep a copy of this document*, which is your proof that you purchased an item via the magazine. If your supplier goes out of business before your order is fulfilled and the magazine subscribes to the MOPS (Mail Order Protection Scheme) the magazine is then liable under MOPS to make up your losses.

If you need to have your order fulfilled quickly and have already discussed this with the retailer, make a note to that effect across the order – the suggested wording is 'to be delivered on (insert date here) as discussed with (insert salesperson's name here). Time is of the essence in this contract.' If there are any problems and delivery is delayed this wording gives you the option of cancelling the contract.

The preferred method of payment is by credit card. If the retailer goes out of business the credit card company is liable for your loss as long as the cash price of the individual item you are buying is more than £100. There are exceptions to this rule: corporate credit cards and purchases made by anyone other than the named card-holder will not be covered by the credit card company. Transactions made from companies registered overseas should be covered as the major credit card issuers have agreed to meet these claims. In general, this method of payment gives you near cast-iron protection against a supplier going out of business or not fulfilling your order for any other reason.

If paying by credit card, make sure that you will not be charged until the goods are despatched. It is not unheard of for companies to take an order for goods that are out of stock, take the money immediately and then fulfil the order a month or two later when the goods arrive in their warehouse.

Also check whether a credit-card surcharge will be added to your bill. Many smaller suppliers (and even a few larger ones) do this to offset the commission they have to pay the card company for each card-based transaction. Make sure you know where your supplier stands on this before telling them your card number.

Most retailers also now accept debit cards (e.g., Switch, Delta). These give you *no protection at all*. Beware – some retailers will try to charge you a surcharge on these as well. Debit cards are not liable to the same surcharges as credit cards, they do not offer you the same degree of protection and they cost the retailer a fixed transaction fee, exactly like a normal cheque. If you have to pay by debit card (and this is not recommended unless you have no other option) make sure that you get an assurance that a credit surcharge will not be added to the bill. You may need to argue this point strongly. If your retailer insists on applying the surcharge, go elsewhere.

If your retailer is local, you may prefer to pay by cash and pick up the goods yourself. This could save you the delivery charge (usually not more than £20 or so) and may give you the option of negotiating a better price. Not all retailers accept personal calls, and not all prefer cash sales.

If you decide to collect the goods yourself, ask if you can see your system working before you take it away. Apart from peace of mind, this also gives you a chance to see for yourself how to connect up the different parts of your computer. For a beginner this can be a major confidence booster. It is also a chance to ask the support staff any simple technical questions.

Unfortunately only smaller retailers are able to provide this level of personal service. Some, although not all, larger companies tend to keep their sales and delivery teams well apart from their engineering and support staff. If you are dealing with one of these it is far more likely that you will be presented with a stack of boxes.

If you run a medium-sized business it can be worth trying to pay on account – 30-day terms are often possible if you can supply trading references. This offers all the usual advantages of improved cash flow, but these have to be offset against the amount of work you need to do to set up an account in the first place. If you are likely to be using a single retailer for most of your computer equipment purchases it can be advantageous to arrange an account facility.

When the goods are delivered write 'Goods not yet inspected' on the consignment note. This improves your legal standing if you need to return the goods for any reason. Inspect your order as soon as possible and, if you have any queries, contact the salesperson responsible for your order immediately. Follow this up with written confirmation of any defects or missing items as soon as you can.

Teething troubles

Not all costs are financial. You will also have to spend some time setting your system up once it has arrived and dealing with any teething troubles that arise.

Even for a small, single-user computer system, you should allow at least a day after the machine arrives for checking and general setting-up. This should give you enough time to become familiar with the system and work out how all the parts link together. If you are a relative newcomer, allow at least a week before you think about using the system professionally. This gives you time to make mistakes without worrying about the consequences. It also gives you a chance to get to grips with the software.

The best way to avoid problems is to choose your dealer wisely. A good dealer will be more likely to sell you a machine that has been fully set up and less likely to misbehave. *Skimping on good support is a false economy.* By the time you have allowed for your time, a cheap system can prove to be far more expensive than one with excellent support that costs that bit extra.

Even the best dealer will sometimes make a mistake and you may be left with a system that does not function properly. At this point the time you have put into looking for good support will pay off. If your computer does not work, double-check all the connections. If everything is as it should be, call the technical support number and explain what the problem is. At this point you are still covered by the Sale of Goods Act 1979 and subsequent amendments. It is the supplier's responsibility to provide a product that is fit for the purpose for which it is purchased. If the product does not do the job the supplier has to give you your money back or at least to put the problems right at his or her cost.

When telephoning, make a note of the name and position of the person to whom you spoke. This gives you a chance to establish a personal contact inside the company. Explain the problem, make a careful note of any solutions they suggest and then try them out. You will have a much better case if you do this as soon as you can. If, after a week or so of trying, your computer is not functioning properly, consider taking the matter up with the company director(s) and – if necessary – ask for a full refund.

JUST WHAT CAN YOU EXPECT FROM MOPS?

In theory MOPS should protect you if a retailer ceases trading. In practice, however, most magazines limit themselves to a fairly low ceiling on compensation payments: £30,000 for any given retailer, and up to £100,000 in any given year.

Realistically, therefore, MOPS is best thought of as a last resort. Your first line of attack should always be to take up the claim with the company's receiver, and then with your credit card company. If you are paying for your purchase with a loan or with extended credit you may also find that you are insured against non-delivery of the goods. The details will be in the small print of your agreement. If this is the case you will also need to register a claim with your loan or credit supplier.

MOPS awards are *discretionary*, which means that there is no legal and binding obligation on the part of the magazine to pay you more than they think is reasonable. A large computer retailer may receive hundreds of orders a day, and may be trading on the verge of bankruptcy for weeks, or even months. A payout of a few tens of thousands of pounds will not amount to much if it has to be split between thousands of buyers. Although you may be lucky, especially if you are dealing with a small retailer, the harsh truth is that it is unwise to expect more from MOPS than a token compensation payment.

CHAPTER 12

FINDING EFFECTIVE SUPPORT

THE MAJORITY of computer problems are minor and easy to put right: for example, you lose your last few minutes' work. Every once in a while, however, something serious goes wrong.

Problems fall into three categories: user errors, software problems and hardware problems.

User errors

These happen when you try to do something your software was not designed to do. Often the software simply does not work the way you think it should. (This is a very common problem.) Most user errors are caused by insufficient training or bad software design. There is very little you can do about bad software design, other than choosing your software carefully. Good training and support can prepare you to deal with further problems. If you are a complete beginner training and support are *not* options. Very little software is clear and simple enough for a novice to pick up on the spot. Training can help you find and use all the features your software can offer you (according to one estimate, most users are familiar with around 20 per cent of the features in a typical office word-processing package).

Software problems

Unfortunately, software is not infallible. In fact, by the reliability standards of any other trade, some software is really rather poor. Even the best programs are about as reliable as an old car on a frosty morning. Most of the time they work well, but occasionally they will do something unexpected or refuse to work at all.

Software problems – known colourfully as **bugs** – take various forms from the obvious (your computer stops responding – this is known as a crash, and the computer is said to have hung), to the extremely subtle (information starts to disappear for no good reason). There is very little you can do to protect yourself from bugs.

To date, the software industry has managed to survive without proper consumer resistance to its bad reliability record. If washing machines, cars and video recorders were sold with the same reliability problems the public outcry would be deafening. The unprofessional attitude to quality control of some of the major companies stems from the industry's roots in the hobbyist movement of the 1970s. Hobbyists – and this includes many computer professionals, who started out as hobbyists – are happy to work around problems, but consumers should not have to. A number of individuals and companies have taken legal action against software providers, but these are usually settled out of court in great secrecy. If the details were made more widely available it is likely that more actions would follow.

If you have software that does not work properly or causes serious problems, you should complain in the same way you would with any other product. If more consumers take action the industry will be forced to sit up and take notice, and the quality of its products will improve. Companies do respond to direct action. In late 1994 the Intel Corporation, which makes computer chips for most IBM-compatible computers, climbed down from what many felt was the high-handed position it had taken with regard to a defect in one of its chips. Intel denied there were problems, but then apologised after a month of vociferous complaints and threats of legal action from angry consumers and went on to offer a free lifetime replacement to anyone who bought a computer with a defective chip. Similar action by software users could revolutionise the industry.

In the meantime, you can expect regular problems with many common software packages. Some features will not work as advertised, others will cause error messages to appear on the screen, and very occasionally you will find software that crashes your computer. Increasing familiarity with the software will confirm that these kinds of problems are not a result of user error. But until consumers start to demand an acceptable standard of performance from the software manufacturers, problems such as these will remain a fact of life.

You should make sure that you register your software when you buy it. This necessitates filling in a short questionnaire that comes with the package and sending it to the manufacturer. Most software is regularly updated, with combinations of fixes for problems and new features. If you register you are more likely to be informed of these updates when they become available. Sometimes you may even be eligible for free updates.

Setup and installation problems

Before you can use your computer both the hardware and the software have to be fully installed. This is one area which can cause problems for beginners, and if not done correctly it can affect the performance of the whole system. If you have bought the system from a dealer, the dealer should do this for you. A scrupulous dealer will make sure that everything has been installed correctly. However, not all dealers bother and as a result you may get a computer that appears to work, but which may not have the full range of options available. You can avoid these kinds of problems by choosing your dealer carefully.

Hardware problems

Hardware problems are rare. Most computer hardware works reliably most of the time, and you are unlikely to come across hardware problems if your system has been set up properly. When they do occur, however, they are serious and can render your computer useless.

Typical hardware problems include:

No power You turn on the power switch, and nothing happens.
No hard disk The power comes on, but the hard disk does not work, or it appears to work, but all the information has disappeared.

No picture The computer whirrs and beeps, but nothing appears on the screen.

No keyboard and/or mouse The computer does not respond when you type or when you move the mouse. This can often be a software problem, but if you turn your computer off and on again and the symptoms remain it is a hardware problem. Also check all cables and plugs. Is everything plugged in properly? Are any of the connecting cables loose? Is there anything lying on the mouse?

Hardware problems require expert attention, and it is at this point that support is most needed and any warranties, insurance policies and maintenance contracts you have taken out will prove their worth.

CASE HISTORY: Andrew

Andrew Thomas, an independent computer consultant, is familiar with computer crises of all kinds.

'*The most common problem I deal with is rogue software. I train all my clients to use the tools effectively, but I still have to field complaints from them when the software bombs or misbehaves. I warn clients in advance about the problems they'll meet. Each package has its own quirks, and I've started avoiding some of the less reliable ones because it's not worth my time trying to explain to clients what the problems are. Some of the bigger packages can do a hell of a lot, but if they're not totally reliable, they can be more trouble than they're worth.*

'*Occasionally I'll have to deal with a big hardware failure. It's not something I can guarantee against, so I make sure that there's always a proper warranty or support policy involved. But I'm often called in to pick up the pieces afterwards. In one case a newsagent lost all his information when his hard disk failed. It literally disintegrated. I opened the case up at home and all that was left was some fine dust and a few small pieces. He was covered by a warranty and had a replacement fitted the next day. But he couldn't get the safety copies of his work back on to it.*

'*In his case it was easy to sort out, and everyone got their papers as usual the next day. Sometimes it's not quite so easy. But if you keep backups of your information and have a good support or insurance policy then you're pretty much bomb-proof no matter what happens.'*

Training

Good training minimises your software support requirements, helps you to make effective use of your software and builds your confidence. It will also help you avoid bad habits. Many packages allow you to get the same result in different ways. Training can help you find the way that works best for you. It can also show you useful tricks, such as how to undo your last action if you make a mistake.

There are two kinds of computer training. The first relates to specific software. This will teach you how to do specific tasks – lay out a page in a word processor, check the spelling of the text, and so on – for a certain product.

The second and perhaps more useful option is one that offers general computer literacy. This teaches you the skills you need to use any commonly available piece of software. It is a much broader level of training, and one that can help you become more self-reliant in the way that you use computers.

Sources of training include:

- manufacturers' training programmes
- independent training programmes
- dealers
- college or night school
- books and videos.

Training programmes run by software manufacturers tend to be expensive. You get extra support and a guarantee that the training will get the best out of the software you have. But this level of support tends to be corporate in both approach and cost and is not suitable unless you run a medium-sized business and have cash to spare.

Manufacturers usually use external training companies. Sometimes these companies go through a certification process which guarantees a certain level of competence, both in the subject and in training ability in general. This should – in theory

– improve your chances of being taught properly. In practice training can be a personal thing, and you need to find a training environment in which you feel comfortable. A beginner's first steps in computer literacy can be nerve-wracking, and it is important to find training that can support you through this phase.

Independent trainers vary considerably. At one end of the scale there are the smaller consultancy and training services which offer affordable and friendly help for anyone starting out. At the other end there are larger training companies who are geared more towards corporate accounts and charge accordingly. There is no lack of training options available – as always the *Yellow Pages* is a good place to start – and after some initial enquiries you should be able to find someone who is offering their services at the level you require.

Getting training and help from a dealer can be much more problematic. Only the larger explicitly business-oriented dealers offer this level of service, and even then they may simply recommend a local training service with which they have good links. Unless you are getting a package as an all-inclusive service from a consultant, you will often be better off doing the research yourself and finding a source of training that suits you, rather than your dealer.

Training at college or evening classes has its advantages. You will get a chance to practise in a relatively unpressured environment and may be given access to computer equipment outside class hours. This can be an excellent place to start if you know nothing at all about computers and want to learn the basics. Many colleges run classes in business-related computing which can give you practical experience of business software. Attending one of these before you buy your system can give you some insight and knowledge to enable you to make a wiser purchase. You may even be able to ask your tutor for help or free buying advice.

The only disadvantage of college courses is that the content is often determined by the software the college supports. Larger training organisations cover most of the software options that are available, and college courses can sometimes although not always be more limited in their scope. You may find that you learn to use software that turns out not to be right for you. Fortunately the basic skills you gain can usually be transferred to another package.

Some office-skills teaching organisations offer basic courses in various word-processing programs. These tend to teach very much by rote, rather than giving you the wider background you need to be truly computer-literate. But if you are not worried about using your computer to do anything other than certain kinds of work you may find them a good choice.

Finally, some people find the do-it-yourself approach appealing. There is no lack of books, magazine features and videos offering help and guidance in computer techniques. Working from the printed page or television screen enables you to go at your own pace and to make mistakes without feeling self-conscious, but the usefulness of these training materials varies hugely and if you get stuck you have no one to ask for help.

Your best approach to choosing training materials is to browse as thoroughly as you can. You may find that some styles are distracting. Many computer books are written with a humorous edge, which suits some people; others prefer a no-nonsense style. (Books for the computer user are discussed in more detail on pages 253–4.)

When it comes to videos, your choices are more limited. If at all possible you should ask for a demonstration or sample video to get some idea of each company's approach to the subject. Ideally you should also be able to look at videos on approval, although for obvious reasons most video sources are unwilling to allow this. Avoid gimmicky videos. It is all very well having famous names on a training video, but you are paying for information and educational content and should assess it on that basis. Video training is advertised in most of the computer magazines.

CASE HISTORY: Beth

Beth Waites ran through most of the available training options when she was starting her carpet-cleaning and house-valeting business. Her experience shows that expensive training is not always the best.

'We'd budgeted for a good computer for the bookkeeping and promotional work, and I knew I needed help to get started. We bought a budget machine on the advice of a friend, so we didn't expect much in the way of help from the dealer. It was obvious I was going to have look elsewhere.

'I started with a magazine feature on business training. But that looked too heavy for me. And the prices were outrageous. There was no way that I was going to pay £1,000 for a week away, even if it was in a plush venue. The subject matter didn't suit either. I wanted to know how to design flyers and leaflets and make our correspondence look professional, and wasn't fussed about pivot points in spreadsheets or graphical trend analysis. I leave that kind of thing to our accountant.

'I tried the local college, and that looked promising. The courses looked right, but I had missed the start of the next one and didn't have a year to spare waiting for the one after. But I talked to the course tutor, and he let me on anyway. By then I'd missed the basics, so after the first couple of classes I felt like giving up. But the tutor suggested a couple of books, so I went out and got those and started working through them at home.

'Now, this worked. They were done as tutorials, so I could start at the beginning and work my way through. Every so often I'd get stuck and I'd ask the tutor to help me out at the next class. Between us we managed to cover everything I wanted to know, and I definitely feel I've mastered the basics now.

'I didn't try videos. I've always preferred to talk to a real human being. Books are cheaper and tell you just as much, but without the pictures. If I was doing it again I'd follow the same route – books and maybe magazines, together with evening classes. It worked for me and I'm not exactly Einstein when it comes to these things, so I think anyone should be able to do it.'

Software support

Unlike training, software support is more of a continuing investment. Ideally, if you have sorted out your training needs properly, then you will be left needing minimal support. This is the best possible – and often cheapest – position to be in. In practice of course you may come across situations that you haven't been prepared for, and this is where support becomes essential.

Like training, software support is available from a number of sources, including:

- manufacturers' support lines
- independent telephone support services
- consultants and friends and colleagues
- dealers
- computer clubs
- on-line services.

Manufacturers' support schemes

If you buy software from one of the big names (Microsoft, Lotus, Novell and so on) then you will be eligible for access to their help lines. Unfortunately, this is not always as useful as it sounds.

Some manufacturers now charge for technical support, so you will not be able to get help and advice unless you pay in advance. Others offer free support for a 'running-in' period – usually 90 days – and charge after that. Check the details when you buy software. Free initial support is definitely worth taking up but a paid-up scheme that ties you to any one manufacturer is *not* a good deal. Manufacturers' own-brand support schemes tend to be expensive and will not always offer you the service you need. Sometimes one manufacturer will blame another for the problems you are experiencing. If you contact the other manufacturer they may point the finger back. From a support point of view you are left floundering. It is worth remembering too that technical support lines of major software manufacturers can get very busy, and you could be kept on hold. While free services are worth taking up, paid support contracts from any one manufacturer are best avoided.

Independent support services

A much better solution is to use one of the independent technical support lines. These cover all the standard packages. They can help with problems that you may have getting different software packages to work with each other.

There are two kinds of support schemes. The first gives you a premium rate telephone number. When you need support, you call the number. You can call as often as you like, for as long as you like, but remember that you pay by the minute for this kind of help. In general, such support schemes are recommended if you simply need occasional help with occasional problems and are confident with your computer. If you have sorted out your training, you may find that this is all the help you need and it will also provide you with a cost-effective way to get access to professional help when you are unable to work out what to do on your own.

The other option is the flat-rate scheme. This can be expensive – perhaps £100 for a year's support – but you will be able to ask all the questions you need and will also have the benefit of support for a wide range of industry-standard software. This circumvents the 'It's not us – it's some other software' problem that besets some manufacturers' support facilities.

Some schemes offer a sliding scale, whereby you get access to better support by paying more per year. Training is a better way to spend your money than on this kind of open-ended support. A recent development are combined support and insurance services. These can be very good value, although it is prudent to check in the usual way that both the insurance and the support facilities are up to par.

The managing director of a large company that provides a variety of PC support services, including support lines for a number of monthly computer magazine titles, explains what the services include.

'We find that 80 per cent of problems are manual related. People simply haven't read the manual or had the training they need. But we're not here to train people, just to solve specific problems.

'We work according to very definite guidelines. We're open 24 hours a day, 365 days a year. Our busiest day last year was Boxing Day – it's when everyone is trying their new kit out – and we were ready for that. We guarantee to answer the phone within six rings, which means we always keep an adequate level of cover.

'When people phone us they're usually irate and frustrated, so the first thing our staff are trained to do is to calm them down.

If you've got a problem you don't want to be messed around with tone phones, you want a real person to talk to right away. Our staff are taught to identify the problem. This isn't always what the caller thinks it is. If a printer's not working it may just be that it's not switched on, so our staff will check all the options.

'If we can't solve it right away, we guarantee to call people back within ten minutes. We have a database of problems that we can refer to which has all the common problems and their solutions. If that doesn't help we keep copies of all the software we support so we can call up the real live version and try things for ourselves.

'I'd suggest to anyone looking for phone support that they check response time, the number of packages that are supported and whether support is available all the time.'

Consultants and other help

If you have arranged for an all-in-one deal with a consultant, then your consultant should be your first port of call when you need support. You may also be able to call up a consultant and ask for help with a specific problem. Some consultants are unwilling to do this unless the problem is major and is likely to require a large amount of time to put right.

As with buying, a good source of help is from friends and colleagues. It is very rare to come across problems that have never occurred before, and you will often find other people have encountered and perhaps dealt with your difficulty already.

Informal support from dealers

You may, if you are lucky, be able to find a dealer who can answer your questions for free. Some dealers see this as part of the service they offer, others as an unwarranted intrusion on their time. If you have chosen your dealer prudently you should be able to get a basic level of help. It is unrealistic to assume that your dealer should know everything about every possible piece of software, but for hardware-related problems a call to your dealer should be your first choice.

Computer clubs

Local computer clubs tend to be the domain of hobbyists and this does not suit everyone who is in need of support. However, they can be a good source of useful advice and information.

There are also two national support groups: the PC Users' Group (PC-UG) and the MacWorks Club for Apple users. Both offer support on a more or less non-profit basis and take a keen interest in keeping users happy. Both groups offer buying support (although the PC-UG does not advise on hardware) as well as a range of other services. Although also dealers, these groups are explicitly consumer-oriented and are a good source of unbiased help and advice.

The PC-UG also prints a monthly newsletter, *Connectivity*, sells its own brand of insurance, maintains an on-line bulletin board service (which includes Internet access) and runs regular training courses and conferences in London. It can also supply information about training organisations. Membership fees are very reasonable.

On-line services

Some on-line services, such as CompuServe and the Internet, include areas where you can ask for computer advice. The advice is free as it comes from other users. (Parts of this book were written with the help of complete strangers on the Internet who were able to provide detailed technical information.) If you already have an on-line connection, or are considering one, then you should investigate this kind of support. However, you need a certain basic level of technical literacy to start to make use of the system, or at least access to someone who can set up a connection for you, and there are no guarantees that you will get an answer to your problem. In practice you usually do, especially for the more commonly asked questions.

Another on-line resource is the FAQ (Frequently Asked Questions) document. This is exactly what it claims to be – a list of common questions, with useful answers. FAQs are maintained on an informal, volunteer basis and there is no guarantee that the information is correct, although technical FAQs are usually maintained by experts and mistakes are soon corrected. FAQs are regularly posted to newsgroups on the Internet. (For more about on-line resources see Chapter 6 and Appendix VIII.)

A BEGINNER'S GUIDE TO HARDWARE

WHAT FOLLOWS is a guide to specifications, which will help you understand computer advertising and compare like for like. Readers who are not interested in technicalities can skip this section and simply quote the recommended hardware specification of their chosen software. If you are interested in games or multimedia titles, then use these as your base specifications, as these applications will need more powerful hardware than business applications.

Many advertisements for computers are little more than a list of technical specifications, which mean less than nothing to many people. Since 1993 any new Apple or IBM-compatible computer has been more than powerful enough for basic business use. If this is all you need a computer for, you are spoiled for choice.

Like cars, however, computers come in economy and performance versions. Performance computers go faster, and – surprisingly, perhaps – are better suited to play than work. Computer games and leisure products tend to put much higher demands on machines than basic business software.

Most of the information in this Appendix applies to IBM-compatible machines. These are often sold on the basis of a specification, rather than as a brand name. The fact that a computer is made by IBM, Dell, Gateway or any other supplier tells you very little about its performance – although it may offer some hints about build quality and support – and marketing titles such as 'Premier' or 'Executive' are simply window-dressing. What matters is what is inside the box, and it is now traditional to list a certain basic set of specifications so that buyers can see what they are getting.

The situation is slightly different with Apple machines, because these are sold more as commodities. The number of Apple suppliers is much smaller, and the market is much less competitive. For the sake of comparison, however, some of the basics – processor type and speed, memory and hard disk size and so on – are often quoted anyway. The two ranges are not strictly comparable, and you should still take the time to sit down and try out each kind of machine for yourself before you buy. However, you can use this section and the one that follows to understand specifications for either kind of machine.

The processor

This is the technical name for the main chip at the heart of your computer. This chip does most of the work and its speed and power largely determine the capabilities of the machine as a whole. The rest of the hardware exists to get information into and out of this chip.

The chips themselves are square ceramic slabs with hundreds of tiny pins. The top surface is printed with the chip model number. The underside contains the pins arranged around a sliver of processed silicon which is visible in the centre through a glass window. This sliver does the work. The chip is in fact a tiny circuit board, with microscopic circuit elements etched into place using a variety of chemical processes.

The most important thing about a processor is its model number (286, 386, 68040 and so on). Associated with the model number is an optional modifier tag such as SX, DX or SLC, and a speed rating (e.g., 25 or 66). The modifier tells you the sub-class of the chip. Sub-classes differ slightly in efficiency and the features they offer. On IBM machines, for example, SX chips are usually hobbled in some significant way to provide a cheaper alternative to DX chips which are the fully working versions.

The model number, modifier and speed rating tell you everything there is to know about a chip and give you a very good foundation for assessing the power of the computer as a whole.

IBM processors

One company – Intel – has been associated with the IBM-compatible product line from the beginning. As machines have become more powerful, each development has become synonymous with one particular kind of Intel chip. So a computer built around a 386 chip is simply known as 'a 386'. A complete list of Intel chips is shown in the table on page 166.

All processor chips use the standard speed rating system. This is measured in MHz (MegaHertz – millions of ticks a second) and this indicates the 'heart rate' of the machine, also known as the clock speed.

The higher the speed rating, the faster the chip works. Each chip model is available in a range of speeds. For example '486' chips are available in speeds from 25MHz to 100MHz. '386' chips cover the range from 16MHz to 40MHz.

Chip speed is similar to engine capacity in a car. A two-litre model will be faster than a one-litre design, but never twice as fast. The same applies to computer chips: a computer built around a 66MHz chip will not run twice as fast as one based on a 33Mhz chip, but it will run noticeably faster.

Recently Intel has started to face stiff competition from various other chip manufacturers. This will result in a range of machines that are advertised as Pentium class and will compete directly with the very latest and fastest Pentium chip that Intel released in 1994. The difference between these and 'true' Pentium designs should be non-existent, although there is a good chance that competing chips will be significantly cheaper.

To counteract this attack on its market share, Intel has coined a slogan – 'Intel Inside' – in an attempt to become the de facto standard. In practice, repeated tests have shown that Intel chips are not noticeably faster or better than comparable chips supplied by its competitors. As a buyer there is no good reason to stick exclusively to 'Intel Inside' machines. You may in fact find that competing machines offer a better price/performance ratio.

Overdrive processors

On many IBM models you can change your processor chip to another one of the same family that goes faster. So, for example, if your computer uses a 486SX/25 chip, you can remove it and replace it with a 486DX2/66 chip.

An overdrive processor from Intel can be added to the existing chip to give it a speed boost. Although these are sold as an upgrade, an overdrive chip simply takes over from the old chip. The old chip is left in place and the overdrive chip works around it. Overdrive chips are not good value. If you need a better processor, buy a better processor – sell the old one (if you can) and plug in the new one in the same space. This will give you extra computer power for much less cost.

Apple processors

The processors used in Apple computers are made by Motorola. Motorola has developed its chips in a much more straightforward way than Intel, and the chips used in Apple computers are not available in the same bewildering variety of speed and performance options. A list of Motorola chips is shown below. Motorola and Intel chips are not strictly comparable, but the table does offer a guideline when trying to assess equivalent performance.

Model designation		Performance rating
Intel	Motorola	
8088/8086	68000	Vintage*
80186		(never made available to the public)
80286	68020	Very dated*
386SX	68030LC	Crippled dated chip*
386DX	68030	Full specification dated chip*
486SX		Recent chip*
486SLC		Low power recent chip, used in portable computers*
486DX, DX/2	68040	Entry level chip
486DX/3, DX/4, DX/5		Faster versions of basic 486DX

Pentium	PowerPC	Established chip range
Pentium Pro		Next generation leading edge model

* Now only available second-hand

And the rest?

Two companies, Cyrix and AMD, are now selling their own versions of the most popular Intel chips. Although these are not true copies – that would be illegal – these chips are similar enough to be used as replacements. Indeed, at the time of writing Intel is no longer making the 486 range, and these chips are now only available from other manufacturers. Although these have slightly different names to the usual Intel chips, the same speed rating system applies.

The Cyrix 5x86 chips are equivalent to fast 486 chips, with subtle design improvements that make them work even more quickly. The difference are small and are not worth paying extra for, although these chips are sometimes sold at a discount which makes them good value. Cyrix 6x86 chips are equivalent to Pentiums. They are not quite as speedy at numerical calculations, although they are faster for every other kind of work. If numerical work is important to you, it is a better idea to get a machine that uses a true Pentium.

The AMD 5x86 (although the name is the same, the manufacturer is different) is another improved 486 design, and the same notes and suggestions apply. The 5K86, AMD's version of the Pentium, is more closely equivalent than the Cyrix design. The only distinguishing feature between this and a true Pentium is cost.

In a volatile marketplace, it is impossible to predict what effect these chips will have on overall prices, but Pentium prices are already much lower than might be expected and further promotion of these chips from the competition is likely to push them even lower.

The future

Not only does the industry move fast, but developments are speeding up. As new models are released the older chips move down the table. At the time of writing, the 486 chip range is about to become obsolete, and the Pentium range is set to become the beginner's standard (known in the trade as the entry level).

For light business use all these developments can be quietly ignored. The kind of software used in a typical small business places minimal demands on a 486 chip, never mind a Pentium. If, however, you plan to do advanced work which involves video or sound, or play the latest games, then you will need to keep up with the technology.

Apple computers are now based on a chip range called the PowerPC, the result of co-operation between IBM, Apple and Motorola. This chip has been evolving into a new design called the Common Hardware Reference Platform (CHRP), which will be able to run software for both IBM-compatibles and Apple Macs on the same hardware. At the moment, CHRP is a speculative project, although it has the support of many of the larger names in the industry. If the CHRP standard is accepted it could revolutionise the computer trade, although it is far too early to tell if this is likely to happen.

Monitor/screen

Monitor is just another word for screen – the part of your computer that displays information while you work. The monitor is one of the most important parts of your computer system. It is essential to choose a model that does not cause eyestrain.

To some extent specifications are something of a sideline with monitors. *Never buy a monitor without checking display quality first.* This will tell you far more about whether or not you can live with it on a daily basis than any number of facts and figures. However, specifications can be useful. Various factors in the specification to watch for include:

MPR II certification ensures that whatever other features it has, your monitor produces as little stray radiation as possible and also has a usable minimal performance.

Dot pitch is the size of each dot on the screen. The smaller the dot size, the sharper and clearer the image. Some monitor manufacturers use a 0.30mm dot pitch. Avoid these. Aim for at most a 0.28mm pitch – the current standard. If you can afford it, a monitor with a 0.26mm pitch will give an even crisper image.

Scan rate tells you how rapidly the screen flickers. Anything below 72Hz tends to cause eyestrain. One essential point to check is whether this scan rate is interlaced or not. A non-interlaced monitor gives you a solid picture. Interlacing effectively halves the scan rate, so a 60Hz interlaced monitor will flicker 30 times a second. Most people find this unbearable, even for short periods. Avoid interlaced monitors if you can.

Screen size Monitors are available in a range of sizes. Like television screens, they are measured diagonally from corner to corner. However, not all of the screen area may be available. It is not unusual for a black frame to appear around the image and this can decrease the available screen size significantly. So you should ask whether or not the monitor has a *full-screen display* or not.

Most monitors are 14 inches wide. If they meet the specifications given above these are perfect for everyday business use.

Larger monitors are a useful, although hardly essential, extra. They often offer improved image quality and can also display more information at once. When working with lots of applications a 14-inch-wide screen can sometimes start to look cluttered. This is less of a problem with larger monitors.

Current 'large' sizes include 15-inch, 17-inch, 20-inch and 21-inch. The 20-inch-plus monitors are expensive (typically well over £1,000) and ideally suited for work which involves the manipulation of images on-screen, such as professional-quality DTP, graphic design and image retouching.

The 17-inch designs are aimed at the more serious computer user who needs to have the extra flexibility that a larger monitor offers. They are excessive for everyday business use, but are very useful for DTP.

The 15-inch models are aimed at users who have some spare cash and would like to improve their computer systems slightly.

The extra inch makes a small but noticeable difference to a computer's ease of use. It is not usually worth spending the extra unless you have tried the monitor first and discovered that there is a good reason why you need the extra area.

Resolution tells you how much detail the screen can show. The more dots there are available, the finer the image becomes. A good minimum to watch for is the SVGA standard, which is 640 dots across and 480 dots vertically. Each dot can be one of 256 colours. This is enough to reproduce photographs with some semblance of realism. Other typical sizes are 800 x 600 and 1024 x 768. You will need a larger monitor to make use of these.

The number of available colours also varies. The minimum is 16 and is best avoided. 256 is now the standard. 64,000 and 16.7 million are the other common options. The latter is particularly worthwhile, as it is good enough to reproduce colour photographs accurately.

As the number of colours goes up, the scan rate goes down, because the computer has to shift much more information to create each picture. If you plan to work with photographs or artwork, ask to see the monitor working with 16.7 million colours as well as the standard 256, and check whether the screen flicker is still bearable. Also note that you need a more powerful computer to give a reasonable performance with 16.7 million colours than one which gives the same performance with 256 colours.

By 1996-7 a new generation of solid state monitors is likely to start appearing. These will be based on the same display technology used in portable computers, and will offer excellent flicker-free performance with vivid colours in a much thinner (near-flat) case. However, the prices of these new models are likely to be very high for some while. If money is no object, these are well worth considering. They are much easier on the eyes than conventional monitors and also consume much less power.

One option worth considering on a tight budget is a monochrome monitor. For most office work colour is useful but hardly essential. Typically monochrome monitors cost half the price of the cheapest colour version and offer much better performance in terms of image sharpness and long-term viewability. However, these monitors are now stocked by only a small number of retailers. Colour is certainly appealing, though not essential for some kinds of business work.

The hard disk drive

This is the computer's filing space. Although a typical hard disk unit may be roughly the size of a thick paperback, it will have enough room for more than 400 copies of the text of this book.

Hard disk capacities are measured in megabytes (Mbs) where 1Mb is the space needed to store one million letters or other characters. The more Mbs, the more room the computer has for software, records and other information. 1,000 Mbs is known as a gigabyte (Gb), and multi-gigabyte drives (which are large enough to store long snatches of sound and video) are now becoming common. Disk sizes of 750Mb and upwards are now standard. These offer plenty of space for all but the most demanding users. 540Mb should be considered an absolute minimum, although the difference in price between this and larger sizes is now so small that there is very little reason to settle for less than 540Mb unless your budget is very tight indeed.

For business use Apple machines tend to offer – and need – smaller-capacity hard disk drives than IBM models. As a very rough guide you can expect around half the capacity on a comparable machine. This does not apply to models used for desktop publishing and audio-visual (AV) applications. The latter particularly need gigabyte-sized drives.

Hard disk types

Not all hard disks are the same. There are currently three standards in use. These are known as IDE, Enhanced IDE (EIDE, also known as mode 3 and mode 4), and SCSI (pronounced 'scuzzy'). IDE is an old standard and is limited to disk drives of 520Mb or less. Enhanced IDE is an extension of the same technology and can handle drives in the gigabyte range. SCSI is an alternative system that has been in use for over a decade. It is ideally suited to larger drives and is also slightly faster than IDE or EIDE. All Apple computers use the SCSI system as standard, but are now starting to become compatible with IDE and EIDE as well. This is reversed on PC compatibles. High-performance machines offer Fast-SCSI and Wide-SCSI models. These are available with the same capacities as ordinary SCSI drives but can move information approximately two or four times faster respectively, and are recommended for anyone working with sound and video.

Older machines used the ESDI and ST506 standards. These are now obsolete, and you will not be able to buy new disks that use these standards. If you run out of space on one of these machines you will almost certainly have to buy a new computer.

The floppy disk drive

This is a slot at the front of the computer that takes plastic wafers known as *floppy disks* (usually shortened to *floppies*), which are now rigid not flexible. The information is stored on a thin disk of magnetically sensitive plastic. The tough outer casing protects the sensitive surface from fingerprints, dust and other damage which might destroy the information.

All modern machines include one 3.5-inch 1.44Mb floppy disk drive. This means that you can use two kinds of floppy disk with them – high-density 1.44Mb disks, and older, double-density 720Kb disks which hold half as much information but are significantly cheaper. Either will work in the same slot.

Much older machines use a different kind of floppy disk. These are 5.25 inches across and protect the inner disk with a much thinner floppy plastic sheath. They hold less information (a maximum of 360Kb) and take up more space. Unless you buy a computer with a dual-format disk drive (and these are very rare) or with one of each kind of disk drive (also rare, and now usually available only to order) you will not be able to use either kind of disk in your machine. The two systems are mechanically incompatible.

Some software is still sold on 5.25-inch disks, although these are now all but obsolete. It is moderately straightforward to upgrade from one kind of disk to another, although this will not be possible on very old machines.

Main memory

A computer's memory is rather like desk space in an office. The more you have, the easier it is to have all kinds of documents and other information scattered around without having to look things up in a filing system. If you have too little memory then applications will either not work at all or will slow down dramatically as the computer continually swaps information between the main memory and the hard disk.

Like hard disk space, memory sizes are measured in Mbs. Older models offer 2Mb of memory or less. This is far too little for modern software. Dated models will have 4Mb. This is adequate for modern software, but tends to slow things down. More recent machines are fitted with 8Mb; 16Mb is better. At the time of writing, this will add another £250 or so to the price of a machine, although there are signs that memory prices are set to drop sharply. Only audio and video editing and image retouching software are likely to need more than this. Although 16Mb will speed things up, the difference will not be as dramatic as the difference between 4Mb and 8Mb.

Apple computers tend to offer – and need – more memory than IBM models. Unless you are doing very demanding work you should find that 16Mb on either kind of machine will be ample for any task.

Cache memory

This is extra super-fast memory which acts as a notepad for the processor chip. Cache memory is often used on IBM-compatibles to speed up the rest of the machine. 256Kb is the standard size. Cache memory is almost always supplied with a machine. A system that lacks cache memory will run much more slowly. Since a set of cache chips costs around £40 to fit, you should make sure that a cache is included when you order your machine as it makes a very noticeable difference to performance.

Pentium computers are available with an even faster kind of cache memory, known as a burst-pipeline cache. This becomes important on the faster kinds of Pentium (100MHz and upwards), as conventional cache memory can become too slow to be effective at these speeds.

Some IBM-compatibles are advertised as having a '16K cache'. This is misleading, as it refers to a different cache built into the processor chip. If you do not see a cache of at least 256Kb advertised, then ask for more details. (This does not apply to the extremely fast Pentium Pro range of chips, which have 256K of memory built into the chip – although extra cache is supplied by most manufactueres as well.)

Expansion slots

The IBM PC is an open-ended design, which means that it is easy to add extra features. These plug into slots on the motherboard. As the IBM range has evolved, these slots have evolved with it.

The number and type of slots in your machine set a limit on how many extras you can add. All IBM-compatibles have ISA (Industry Standard Architecture) slots. These are adequate for relatively slow extras such modems and soundcards, but in computer terms they are rather like a 'B' road – adequate for light traffic, but too slow if you want to move information from one place to another in a hurry.

Faster slots use a 'local bus' system. The cards that fit into these slots are connected more or less directly to the processor chip. This gives a super-fast link between the two. At the moment there are two local bus standards: VESA (Video Electronics Standards Association), this is also shortened to VLB (VESA Local Bus); and PCI (Peripheral Connect Interface). VESA is now used in a few 486-based designs. The faster PCI system is used in the latest 486- and Pentium-based machines. PCI looks set to become an industry standard used by IBM-compatible, Apple and other computer manufacturers. VESA is more of an interim measure and is likely to become obsolete by the end of 1996.

Apple machines also use the NuBus system. This is an Apple-only standard that will soon be obsolete, as Apple is expected to switch to the PCI standard.

Controller card (IBM only)

Local bus slots are used for two kinds of extra. The first of these controls the hard and floppy disk system. This is known as a controller card. These cards are always included when you buy your machine.

The make of controller card determines whether your computer uses IDE, EIDE or SCSI hard disk drives. It also provides a handful of useful extra connections, known as parallel and serial ports. These are simply sockets on the back that you can use for almost anything. Traditionally printers are connected to a parallel port and the serial ports are used to connect a mouse and perhaps a modem.

New Pentium computers now almost always include a built-in controller card on the motherboard. This leaves one extra expansion slot free for other uses. Another useful option is the PS/2 mouse system, which again bypasses a controller card and connects a mouse directly to the motherboard. This usually leaves you with one more serial port free than you would have otherwise.

You will sometimes see controller cards specified as having '2HD, 2FD, 2S, 2P'. This cryptic designation translates as 'This card can be used to connect up to two hard disk drives and two floppy disk drives. It also includes two serial ports and two parallel ports.'

Some hard-disk controllers are cached, which means they have extra 'scratchpad' memory. This should make them quicker than uncached designs. However, the Windows operating system includes a utility which has the same effect.

If you plan to use a modem, make sure that the serial ports use the 16550 chip. This is a chip (not the same as the main processor chip) that controls the operation of the modem through the serial port. It is a newer version of the 6850 chip, which can cause problems when used with faster modems. If your modem plugs directly into a slot inside the computer it will almost certainly bypass the serial port and use a 16550 chip.

Graphics card

The graphics card controls what appears on the monitor. It sets the maximum number of colours that you can use, the resolution and the scan rate. New computers are sold with good basic graphics cards that are perfectly adequate for most work. However, if you plan to work with photographs, animations, or a large monitor you may need to upgrade your graphics card to match. Graphics card specifications quote the amount of memory used, but in practice you are better off checking for scan rate, maximum resolution and maximum number of colours available. Better still, ask to see a graphics card in action at its highest resolution with the maximum number of colours it can produce. This should tell you everything you need to know about the speed and clarity of the display

Many graphics cards are **accelerated**. They are built around a special chip that has been designed specially for graphics. This takes some of the load off the main processor chip and makes everything appear on screen much more quickly.

All modern graphics cards use either the VESA or PCI local bus system for maximum speed. Older ISA-based graphics cards are much slower. The difference can be very noticeable. With accelerated graphics most displays appear almost instantaneously. With ISA graphics you can see different items appearing on the screen as the computer draws them. Text appears much more slowly too. When working with a word processor you will be held up slightly every time you change pages.

Apple machines use the NuBus graphics card standard, although it is likely that this will be switched to PCI soon. One attractive feature of Apple computers is the fact that you can have several different monitors connected at a time, with different information on each one. So, for example, you could have a palette of drawing tools on one screen and an image on another. But to do this you will need to install an extra graphics card.

The latest generation of graphics cards includes features which can give on-screen objects in games a convincing three-dimensional appearance. These features are a very optional extra for anyone planning to use a PC for business, although once the industry chooses between the different competing designs and settles on an appropriate standard they will doubtless become essential for dedicated games players.

Accelerators (Apple only)

Some older Apple machines can take plug-in extras which make several kinds of software run faster. These are known as accelerators. Unlike graphics cards, accelerators work with specific software. One popular example is the Photoshop image-editing package.

Accelerator cards are very application-specific, and you should discuss your needs with your dealer before ordering. The market has been shaken by the arrival of the PowerMac computers, which in many cases are faster, or at least comparable to, older computers with accelerator cards fitted. But if you are buying second-hand then you should consider these cards.

Some older Apple machines also have a PDS (Processor Direct Slot) which allows you to add new processor chips when they become available, so you can upgrade an older and slower model to use PowerPC technology. This can be an expensive proposition, however. If you need the fastest machine possible you should consider getting a PowerMac directly, rather than buying a slower model and upgrading later.

Keyboard

On IBM-compatibles, the 102-key keyboard is the standard. This includes extra keys for numbers on the right-hand side and also arrow keys which are used for moving around the screen. Some keyboards feel much more pleasant to use than others. Some people prefer more of a spongy bounce, others a definite 'clack'. This is a matter of personal taste. Try a keyboard before buying it, especially if you are a touch typist. 'Cherry' keyboards made by the Cherry company, are often offered as an optional extra. These are built to a higher standard than budget keyboards. If possible, buy a *weighted* keyboard; these include a metal weight that makes them less likely to slide around the desk as you type.

Microsoft Corporation offers an ergonomic keyboard as an extra, which has the letters set in more accessible positions and also includes a wrist pad – essential if you want to avoid strain during long typing sessions.

Apple models have a range of keyboards, including an ergonomic design of Apple's own which splits down the middle and swivels. When buying an Apple machine it is important to remember that the keyboard is sold as an extra – it will not usually be included in the listed price. One curiosity of older Apple keyboards is that they do not include a separate backspace key – watch out for this when buying second-hand. This has been remedied on all current models.

Cases (IBM only)

IBM-compatible machines are sold in a standard range of case styles; these do not affect the performance of your computer in any way. A big case does not mean a fast and powerful computer, but it does mean you have more room to add extras.

Different kinds of case have different numbers of drive bays – special areas that the extras slot into. Larger cases also have more powerful power supplies to take care of the extra load.

Drive bays are used for extras that need front-panel access – floppy-disk drives, hard-disk drives, tape backup systems and CD-ROM units. Other extras slot into the expansion slots inside the computer's case.

Drive bays come in two sizes – 5.25 inch, which are suitable for 5.25-inch floppy disk drives and CD-ROM players, and 3.5 inch, which are used for 3.5-inch floppy drives and hard-disk drives. When not in use they are screened off with plastic blanking plates. To install an extra you simply remove the plate, slot in the new drive, tighten a few screws and then make the connections to the rest of the computer.

Slimline cases look trim, but are only recommended if you know exactly what you want and are sure you will not need to upgrade. They typically have one of each size of drive bay.

Desktop and mini-tower cases are the most common. The desktop model sits on your desk horizontally and the monitor sits on the case. The mini-tower model stands vertically. These are designed to sit to one side of your desk or perhaps even out of sight under it. Either model will have two of each kind of drive bay as standard.

Full tower cases also stand vertically. They are used for larger computer systems and offer four or five drive bays. These cases are best left on the floor – they are too tall to be used on most desks.

Some cases have a door which closes to hide the drive bays. Unless you are running your computer as a file server, you should avoid this design – the door only gets in the way during everyday use.

And of course, no computer would be complete without a small array of flashing lights and numbers. These will usually include the following:

- a 'power-on' light
- a 'turbo' light (old PC-compatibles had a switch that could change the speed of the computer to make it compatible with slower software. This is redundant now, but seems not to have been removed)
- a hard-disk activity light: this is useful – it tells you when your hard disk is working.

There will also be a handful of buttons. 'Turbo' turns the speed up and down and works with the 'turbo' light. Normally you should leave this button pushed in. You may also see the

---

SPECIFICATION CHECKLIST

Using the recommended system needed to run your software of choice as a guide, you can work out a target hardware specification based on the following:
(1) Apple or IBM
(2) processor chip
(3) memory
(4) floppy disk type
(5) hard disk size
(6) monitor and graphics card: these will be specified as a display standard, such as VGA or SVGA
(7) operating system software: this is included as part of the hardware as they are almost always sold together
(8) all connectors, manuals, mouse and keyboard
(9) optional extras: (i) a printer; (ii) a CD-ROM drive; (iii) a sound-card and speakers; (iv) a modem; (v) a scanner; (vi) networking facilities; (vii) video cards, joysticks and other less usual extras; (viii) backup facilities.

When buying, check each of these items in turn and make sure that all have been included in your order.

Details of the hardware differences between Apple and IBM are discussed in Appendices IV and V.

speed displayed on a large numeric indicator – perhaps as 'HI' and 'LO', or as '66' to indicate 66MHz, '33' to show 33MHz and so on. 'Reset' forces your computer to go through its start-up sequence. *Do not touch this button without a good reason.* You will lose any unsaved work. The reset button should only be used when your computer has obviously 'hung' and needs to be restarted. Switching the power on and off again strains the hardware slightly (although whether or not this makes a lasting difference is debatable). Use the reset button instead.

HARDWARE EXTRAS AND UPGRADES

SOME HARDWARE extras are entertainingly useless, such as a simulated sailing tiller which connects to your computer and lets you practise your navigation skills. Others, such as printers, are all but essential.

Like the other parts of your computer system, each extra has its own specification and jargon. Not all have specifications that are quoted with software. To some extent they depend on personal preference. Fortunately, most extras are relatively straightforward and do not demand the same kind of technical knowledge that computers themselves do.

Printers

If your business needs to make a good impression, it can be well worth taking the time to choose a good printer. The currently available options include:

Daisy wheel These printers are now so rare as to be all but obsolete, but they were popular until the early 1990s and do occasionally appear on the second-hand market. Daisy-wheel printers work by slamming metal dies against a ribbon, which then print letters on to the paper. The dies are arranged in a circle on spokes around a central support. The whole arrangement looks rather like the petals of a flower – hence the name.

Daisy-wheel printers are very slow and very loud and can only produce text – pictures, decorative borders and so on are not possible. Their only advantage is that they can produce true

This is an example of near letter quality (NLQ) mode printing
from a dot matrix printer.

This is an example of draft mode printing
from a dot matrix printer.

This is an example of Times 12 point output on a 300 dpi laser printer.

This is 9 point Times Roman

This is 12 point Courier

This is 14 point Helvetica

This piece of text has been output from a bubble-jet printer.

typewriter-quality print. With the relative affordability of good-quality laser and bubble-jet printers, however, these printers have fallen by the wayside.

Dot matrix 9-pin These printers are the most basic models available. Because the printing system is mostly mechanical (a print head with 9 retractable pins scans across the paper and 'punches' dots on to it) these printers are slow, irritatingly loud and produce poor-quality output. However, they are cheap (a typical example might cost around £100) and have negligible running costs. Apart from paper and minimal electricity consumption, the only extra costs are inked ribbons. These need to be replaced once or twice a year and cost under £10.

These printers are ideal for businesses and sole traders who do not need to have impressive stationery. A 'near letter-quality' mode is available for other kinds of correspondence. This is adequate for light business use, but does not approach the sharpness of the lettering produced by a good typewriter.

Only the simplest block and line graphics are possible with these printers; photographic images are not. The machines can produce a range of lettering styles with appropriate software, but compared with other printers the results can look amateurish and rough.

Dot matrix 24-pin 24-pin printers offer improved print quality over 9-pin printers, but otherwise have the same advantages and drawbacks. They cost between £100 and £150. Near letter quality printing is noticeably better, but the results still look rough compared with a proper typewriter.

Bubble-jet/ink-jet These are the names used by different manufacturers for a machine that works by electrostatically squirting tiny blobs of ink on to a sheet of paper. They are quiet, slightly faster than dot matrix printers and give reasonable results at a modest cost – typically £200 to £400. Running costs are moderate for light use. The ink is supplied in the form of cartridges, which cost about £20 to replace. Ink and re-inking equipment are available if you want to refill cartridges by hand, although this can be messy.

A bubble-jet printed page will always look slightly rough, although the print quality is significantly better than that offered by dot-matrix machines. The quality can be improved by using high-quality paper rather than photocopier paper. This makes the printers suitable for professional work, especially for sole traders working from home. For a start-up business on a tight budget a bubble-jet printer provides the best compromise between cost and print quality. With suitable software, bubble-jet printers can produce different kinds of lettering.

Some bubble-jet printers are capable of colour printing. This can be useful when preparing presentation handouts and creating custom-designed letterheads. Colour, however, is still an expensive extra. Colour pages can cost up to 20p for a page of A4, and it is important to bear in mind that the results from a bubble-jet will be nowhere near photographic quality. For block-colour bar charts and other diagrams however, these printers are by far the best option. Some models can print on overhead transparency film.

Laser Laser printers use a tightly focused beam of light to 'paint' an image on to a special light-sensitive surface. This image is then printed to paper using a system based on photocopier technology. Laser printers give results which approach those possible with conventional typesetting and printing machinery, at a fraction of the cost. A close examination of a laser-printed page will show that the letters are slightly rough compared with work that has been professionally typeset but for many applications the differences are unimportant.

Laser printers are an expensive option. Prices start at around £300 and go up to £2,000 for heavy-duty machines which are capable of serving the printing needs of an entire office.

In addition to the unit price, laser printers are expensive to run. Not only do they consume significantly more electricity than the other printer types, they also require expensive consumables. To produce a laser-printed image, very fine dust-like particles of ink (known as toner) are literally melted on to the page. The toner is supplied in the form of cartridges which need to be replaced every 5,000 pages or so. Toner cartridges can cost up to £100. However, an ink-jet cartridge costs £20 and needs to be replaced every 500 pages.

Another cost can be the replacement of the drum on which the laser writes the image. This is made of a special light-sensitive material which slowly wears out as the printer is used. Drums can cost up to £100 a time. Fortunately these need to be replaced much less frequently than toner cartridges. If you do a lot of printing it can be worth estimating running costs: over the course of a few years consumables can add up to three or four times the original cost of the printer.

Laser printers can handle just about any black-and-white printing task. (Colour laser printers are just starting to become available, but these advanced models still cost many thousands of pounds. It is likely that prices will fall over the next few years, but at present colour laser printing remains a viable option only for large companies with large budgets.) As well as producing different kinds of lettering in different sizes, laser printers can also produce drawings and cartoons. Mid-range and better lasers can also produce good reproductions of black-and-white photographs.

Laser printers are specified according to how finely they can print dots on a page. A low-cost printer can create 300 dots per inch (usually abbreviated to 300 dpi). This is more than adequate for most office work, although lettering produced on a 300 dpi printer does look very slightly rough when compared with professionally typeset printing. 300 dpi lasers are not recommended for photographs. The results are usable for casual dabbling and informal use, but slightly rough for professional presentations.

The next step up is 300 dpi with resolution enhancement. This process fills in the spaces between the dots with smaller dots, creating a sharper result. When buying a laser it is important to check if resolution enhancement is available, as it significantly improves print quality for little, if any, extra cost. However, these printers are still not ideal for work involving photographs.

Higher quality printers can produce 600 dpi. This is useful for low-budget professional publishing work, as the letter quality is sharp and photographs can begin to be reproduced convincingly. Some printers are billed as having a resolution equivalent to 600 dpi. This is simply marketingspeak for a 300 dpi printer with resolution enhancement.

Top-end printers can produce 1200 dpi or better. This begins to approach the results achieved using professional typesetting equipment. Lettering is pin-sharp and photographs can be reproduced realistically. However, these machines are significantly more expensive and are recommended only if your work needs the extra quality. For conventional word processing they are unnecessary.

An important laser-printer specification to watch for is speed. This is specified in pages per minute (ppm.) This is the maximum rate at which the printer can feed paper through. Many lasers do not approach their quoted speeds. Low-cost laser printers can usually manage four pages per minute, which is adequate for everyday business use. More expensive and sophisticated machines offer twice or even three times this rate. These machines are usually designed for heavy-duty work in an office environment where the one printer is shared between many users on a network.

In addition to the printing hardware itself, most laser printers include a sizeable built-in computer of their own to manage the printing process. Like other computers, they need memory to be able to work effectively. Some lasers are supplied with the bare minimum needed to print a single page of A4 text. Graphics, photographs and other styles of lettering may well need more memory than this, and this will have to be bought and installed as an extra. Check with your dealer if you will need to do this based on the kind of work you have in mind. Extra memory can add significantly to the cost of a laser printer.

A range of new printers has gone against this trend. GDI (Graphics Display Interface) lasers use the power of your existing computer (and its built-in memory) to perform the calculations that a standard laser printer does internally. Hence a GDI laser is significantly cheaper and faster than a standard machine, and does not need the extra memory to work at its best. The catch is that GDI lasers will only work with IBM-compatible computers that are running Windows software. MS-DOS software can only print indirectly, by running within a window. Another drawback is that it can be hard to continue using your machine while it is printing – something that does not apply to a properly installed conventional laser.

Laser printers are often advertised as **Postscript-compatible**. Postscript is an image definition system that has become a world standard since it was introduced on the Apple Mac in the mid-1980s. The inclusion of Postscript offers extra facilities and makes a laser printer ideal for use with the many DTP and graphics programs that support this standard.

Dye sublimation, thermal transfer and colour laser printers are all aimed at the professional colour-printing market. They are very expensive, although colour lasers – or laser-like printers – will start to come down in price over the next few years. By the end of the 1990s they are likely to be the new business standard.

Modems

There are three things you should know about a modem. The most important is to check for BABT approval. This means the modem has been through a rigorous program of testing and certification and is fully compatible with the BT network. Unapproved modems are regularly offered for sale and some work well – most of the time. But it is illegal to connect one of these modems to a telephone line, and you are more likely to suffer from minor incompatibility problems (such as not being able to recognise the BT 'busy' signal) than if you buy a fully approved model. Unfortunately the approval process is expensive, and approved models cost slightly more than the unapproved variety. In terms of peace of mind and long-term reliability, however, the extra cost can be worth it. Approved equipment carries the green triangle mark. Unapproved equipment is marked with a red circle.

Next, check whether the modem is internal or external. To install an internal modem you will need to remove the case from your computer and slot the modem into an expansion slot. You are more likely to come across obscure problems while doing this. An external modem is a better choice if you prefer to keep things as simple as possible. You can attach this to your computer with a special cable. Any further setting up should be minimal. When buying an external model, make sure that a cable is included.

Modems work at different speeds. These directly affect your telephone bill, as the faster the modem the more quickly it gets information. Speed is measured in baud or bps (bits per second). Often this is shown as a number − 2,400 for example. These numbers can be compared directly − so a 9,600 modem will move information twice as fast as a 4,800 modem.

A quick back-of-the-envelope calculation shows that a slow modem is not a good buy. Although 2,400 bps modems are now very cheap − around £25 − they are also six times slower than a 14,400 bps modem. So for every hour you spend on-line with the fast modem, you will spend six hours on-line with the slower one and your phone bill will be six times higher. Very slow modems are a false economy. If two computers have different speed modems, the speed at which they will communicate is the highest they can both achieve (e.g., a 9,600 and a 28,800 will talk at 9,600). All modems can talk slower than their quoted rates.

Sometimes speed is shown as a 'v' figure. These are industry-standard codes for different modem speeds and features. The table below lists the most common speeds and typical applications.

Speed	Code	Suggested usage
2,400	V.22bis	Very cheap, but now obsolete and far too slow for everyday use.
9,600	V.32	The bare minimum for regular use.
14,400	V.32bis	A good fast rate for everyday use. Recommended for new users.
28,800	V.34	The fastest modems available and likely to become the new standard by early 1997.
57,600	n/a	Not commercially available or standardised yet, but planned for 1997. Very fast indeed, and pushing the theoretical limit of what the UK phone network is capable of.

Modems are now increasingly being sold as part of an 'Internet kit', which includes the modem itself and a free trial account with an Internet service provider or international on-line service. These kits are not usually a good buy. Free trial accounts are available for the asking from many of the popular service providers, and are often also given away free with magazines. In any case, the provider may not be ideal for your needs. It usually makes more sense to buy a modem separately and then shop around for the best Internet connection on your own terms.

ISDN

British Telecom is now offering subscribers ISDN (Integrated Services Digital Network) connections, which offer a much faster link to on-line services – although not all of these support this new standard yet. ISDN is expensive – the current installation cost is £400, with a line rental of £80 a quarter – but offers two 64,000 bps links. These can be used in parallel to give 128,000 bps, or one channel can be reserved for voice conversations and fax messages and the other for computer use.

While ISDN is out of the financial reach of most home users, it can be a good option for businesses that rely on high-speed access to on-line services, other computers and fax machines. Because ISDN connections are more efficient, any company that sends tens of faxes a day will find the service soon pays for itself.

To use ISDN you will need a 'terminal adaptor' – the ISDN equivalent of a modem. These are now becoming very affordable indeed.

One caveat with ISDN is that it makes much greater demands on a PC. Older, slower machines will not be fast enough to use the service at its maximum capacity. Any mid-price machine bought as new since the summer of 1995 should be up to the task.

Soundcards

These are designed to add sound and music to your computer. All soundcards can record a sound and play it back if you connect them to a microphone and a pair of speakers. This can be useful if you want to add voice annotation to a letter, or if you want to use voice recognition software.

Some also include a music synthesizer. This adds a selection of more-or-less realistic instrument sounds that are used by games and other multimedia software. You will also find many cards that include one or more CD-ROM interfaces. These are connectors you can use when you want to add a CD-ROM drive (see below).

One final extra is a joystick and MIDI Interface. A joystick is a small extra that fits in one hand and is used in games. The MIDI (Musical Instrument Digital Interface) is a computer control system for synthesizers and music keyboards. If you decide the sound from your soundcard is a bit thin, you can add an external synthesizer to make it fuller and richer. If you want to use your computer to record and edit performances from an external music keyboard, you will also need a MIDI interface. (You will also need an adaptor, as the connector on the back of most soundcards does not fit the MIDI standard.)

Over the years a soundcard standard has emerged, based on a range of cards from Creative Labs known as the Soundblaster series. In theory a 'Soundblaster-compatible' card should work with most software that needs a soundcard. In practice this is not always the case. If sound and music are important to you it is well worth getting a genuine Soundblaster card for the best possible results.

Soundcards vary in quality. For sound recording and playback you have a choice between the older 8-bit standard, which is roughly telephone quality, and the newer 16-bit standard, which approaches CD quality. 8-bit recording and playback is adequate for speech. 16-bit playback is used for higher quality music and sound effects.

Sound synthesizers also vary. Older soundcards use the old and very thin-sounding FM (Frequency Modulation) system, which was developed over a decade ago and uses the OPL3 and OPL2 set of chips. Newer soundcards use wavetable synthesis, which uses digital recordings of real instrument sounds, which are much more impressive and lifelike. You can often upgrade older soundcards to wavetable synthesis with a daughterboard. This plugs into a socket on the soundcard and provides better sound.

Amplifiers and speakers

With all soundcards you have the option of piping the sound through your existing hi-fi system. Sometimes it is more convenient to have speakers closer to your computer. Many multimedia systems are sold with speakers which either stand on either side of the monitor or clip on to the sides. Speakers and soundcards are often sold together. When buying a soundcard you should always check if speakers are included. If not, check whether the soundcard has a built-in amplifier. Otherwise you will have to use your hi-fi, buy an external amplifier or buy powered speakers.

Apart from basic sound quality – which only your ears can gauge – it is important to check if speakers are shielded. This means that their heavy magnets will not affect a monitor if placed next to it. Unshielded speakers can damage a monitor, as well as distorting the image on the screen.

Apple multimedia

Sound is slightly better integrated on Apple machines. Many recent models include 16-bit recording and playback as standard. Speakers are either built into the case or the monitor. Synthesizers are not so well catered for, but Apple software tends to get around this by turning the computer itself into a synthesizer.

CD-ROM drives

CD-ROMs look and work rather like conventional CDs, but instead of music, they contain pictures, text, sounds, video clips, software and other kinds of information. To use a CD-ROM you need to install an extra called a CD-ROM drive.

When buying a CD-ROM drive, the most important thing to check for is speed. Originally CD-ROM drives were designed to work at the same speed as music CD players, but this proved slow for computer applications, so double, triple, quad-speed, six-speed and even eight-speed drives started to appear. These shift information into the computer up to eight times more quickly than the original single-speed drives. As they appeared on the market, prices crashed and each new speed increase became a new standard.

Today there is very little reason to buy a double-speed drive when quad-speed drives are only very slightly more expensive. (Single-speed drives are obsolete.) For various technical reasons, six-speed and faster drives are not that much speedier in everyday use, so their extra cost is not usually worth it unless you plan to do a lot of work with CD-ROMs.

All CD-ROM drives can play ordinary music CDs. If you have a soundcard and some speakers, the music will play through them directly – you will not even need to use your hi-fi. The sound quality is not quite up to hi-fi standards, but if you want some music while you work this is adequate. To play music you will also need some appropriate software. This is usually included with the CD-ROM drive itself.

CD-ROMs should also be multi-session. This is specifically for use with the Kodak CD format that stores photographs on a CD. (This service is available as an extra at most high-street film developers.) The CD can be used again and again, so you can keep adding images from a new roll of film until the CD is full. CD-ROM drives that are not multi-session will only allow you to access the pictures from the first roll.

You should also check the connections on your CD-ROM. Sony, Mitsumi and Panasonic are standard (other manufacturers, e.g., Pioneer, use one or other or these), but SCSI and IDE drives are also available. The former need to be connected to a suitably equipped soundcard. The latter use your computer's existing disk controller card.

Finally, some CD-ROMs are video-CD ready. Video-CD is a new format that is supposed to replace pre-recorded video cassettes. It's unclear at the moment whether the standard will survive, or even whether or not users want to watch videos on their computer's screen, but a handful of titles are available and some CD-ROM drives support the standard.

It is possible to buy multi-CD drives. These store a number of CD-ROMs in one unit, and are worth considering if you regularly need to access reference information from a variety of CD-ROMs.

CD writers are just starting to become affordable. Although at the time of writing they still require a sizeable investment, prices are likely to fall below the £500 mark by the autumn of 1996. CD writers look and work like ordinary CD-ROM drives, but can also be used to record information or music onto special gold disk blanks. Dual-speed, quad-speed and combined (quad-speed reading, double-speed recording) models are available, although the quad-speed writing drives do not seem to be perfectly reliable yet.

CD writers require a fast PC that can produce the steady flow of information the writer requires. If the PC hiccups at all the writer will ruin a disk blank. Any medium-price modern PC should be fast enough, but older second-hand models almost certainly won't be.

Other drive types

A number of new data storage options have recently become available, and by the end of 1997 it is very likely indeed that floppy disk drives will become obsolete. Compaq announced in the spring of 1996 that it will be including a special kind of floppy disk drive on some of its new models which can store up to 100 times as much information. Meanwhile, new drives from Iomega and Syquest have also become popular. Two models available from Iomega are the Zip drive, which can store around 100Mb on a cartridge almost exactly the same size as a floppy disk, and the Jaz drive, which stores up to 1Gb on a larger cartridge. These and the similar EZ drives offered by Syquest are relatively affordable and ideal for backups, although of course none has become a standard yet. If you are buying them solely for your own use this is not a worry, but if you are planning to use them to exchange information with friends and colleagues it is too early to tell yet which, if any, of these new systems will become the most popular and widely accepted.

Multimedia kits

It is not unusual to see a CD-ROM drive, a soundcard, some speakers and perhaps some software advertised as a 'bundle'. There is nothing special about this; it uses standard components, but is sold in one box instead of three or four. Sometimes it can be slightly cheaper, but you should still check that all the individual items meet your needs.

Scanners

These copy pictures and photographs directly from a printed page into your computer. The quality range available stretches from simple black-and-white scanning, which is more than adequate for sending paper-based faxes, to full photographic colour. Many scanners come with software for 'optical character recognition' (OCR). This attempts to read a page of text, rather than simply grabbing it as an image – so, for example, the words on the page can be copied into a word processor as if they had been typed. Although the results can sometimes be rough and ready, OCR software combined with a scanner can be a useful time-saving tool for applications where large amounts of text would otherwise have to be typed in by hand. Cheap OCR systems are unlikely to be reliable. You will need a good scanner and good OCR software if you want to use the system professionally. Otherwise, you will have to proofread copy after it has been scanned and make corrections yourself. With a budget system expect an accuracy of 95 per cent at best.

Scanners come in two types. A handheld scanner looks rather like a computer mouse, but bigger and wider. It needs to be held in a special frame as you scan the image by pulling the scanner across it manually. Some are capable of excellent results and can be good value if you only work with images occasionally.

A flatbed scanner is more like a photocopier. You place the image on a glass plate under a lid and the scanner does the rest. These are aimed at the professional user. Some flatbeds also include a transparency adaptor, so you can scan in slides as well as photographs.

Scanners are rated according to colour depth and resolution. The cheapest offer 8-bit greyscale, which means they can resolve 256 shades of grey. The best offer 24-bit colour, which makes them suitable for colour photographs. (A handful of professional-quality scanners offer 36-bit colour which is better still, but only relevant in a professional publishing context.)

Resolutions are specified in dots per inch (dpi) but most scanners use a mathematical process known as interpolation which fills in the gaps between dots and creates a higher effective resolution. 1200 dpi after interpolation is a good basic figure. 2400 dpi is used for more demanding work.

Check also for the TWAIN standard, which is used by most image processing software. This allows the software to work with the scanner more directly.

Mice

A mouse is a hand-held pointing device which fits under your palm. In order to use it correctly the connecting lead should be at the top of the mouse, by your fingertips, as opposed to under your wrist. As you move it from left to right and up and down a pointer on the screen tracks your movements. There are one or more buttons under your fingers at the top of mouse. When you have moved the pointer to an active area on the screen you can make something happen by clicking one of these buttons.

IBM-compatible mice have two or three buttons (although the middle one is usually ignored by most software) and are connected to the computer's serial port, or directly to a special socket on the motherboard (the PS/2 standard). Mice vary mostly on comfort and ease of use. Some are sculptured to fit under your hand, while others are simply blocks of plastic.

Apple mice have a single large button and vary much less. The latest designs are rounded and easy to use. Optical mice use a non-mechanical system to track movements, and are less susceptible to grime and dust. They are not widely available, but seem to be more reliable and long-lasting than the traditional mechanical mouse, and are worth looking out for.

In general one mouse is much like another, and unless you find the one you have been given intolerable, or feel the need to personalise your computer in some way, you will not need to change your mouse for another.

Graphics pads

These are large, flat, plastic surfaces that are used in conjunction with a stylus. The stylus can be used as a pen, so you can draw, write or trace on the pad and the result goes straight on to your computer's screen. It can also be used as a replacement for the standard mouse. Graphics pads are used by artists and illustrators. The best pads are pressure sensitive – as you press harder, the stylus responds. You should always try out a pad for yourself before buying. This is a small market with few competitors. In tests, the most highly rated pads are usually those made by Wacom. Pads are available in sizes from postcard-sized A6 to huge A2. A3 or A4 are adequate for most applications. Larger pads are not necessarily better. If too large you can strain your arms through excessive movement.

Video cards

These use a standard known as MPEG (Motion Picture Experts Group) to make it possible to show full-screen videos on your computer. Without a video card, the image appears in a tiny window on the screen. With the card it can fill the whole screen, and the image will be as detailed as possible.

There are a number of competing video standards on the market. Intel's Indeo system can show full-screen video on a Pentium-based computer without the need for extra hardware. Apple and Microsoft use a system called Quicktime which works in a similar way.

However, some video cards can also be used for image capture. This means they can be connected to a TV or video and will take snaps of the images and store them for later use. Professional-quality cards – called video digitisers – do this fast enough for your computer to record the images as they happen. (The technical term is 'in real time'.) Armed with one of these cards and some suitable software you can use your computer to edit the video.

At the moment it is too early to tell which video standard will prevail, if any. If you need a good-quality video-editing system then opt for one of the professional video digitising cards. The cheaper MPEG-based cards are best seen as an interesting indulgence.

TV tuners

As well as video, it is possible to view TV pictures on your computer. A TV tuner card is simply a TV decoder on a card, with software that displays the images on the screen. These are an entertaining if somewhat expensive novelty. Some include image capture features.

When looking for a TV tuner check if teletext is included. Some portfolio-management software can pick out the latest share prices from the teletext stream automatically to give you an immediate warning of buy and sell conditions. Also check to see how well the software integrates with the rest of the computer. Some TV tuners are less than impressive in this respect.

TV adaptors

TV adaptors take the image that usually appears on a monitor and convert it to a form that can be shown on a TV. They are relatively affordable, and make a good alternative to the very expensive monitor panels that are designed to work with overhead projectors. The main feature to watch for is display resolution and frame buffering – the latter 'locks' the image so it does not flicker on the TV screen.

OPERATING SYSTEMS

MOST SOFTWARE is designed to help you with a specific job — write a letter, send a fax and so on. An operating system, however, works on a more fundamental level. It manages the smooth running of your computer: it takes your commands, passes them on to the hardware and software, and then sends the results back to you.

By choosing the software first you will not need to worry about which operating system to use. It will be given as part of the software's required system specification, together with all the hardware details. Apart from the basics needed to get the software running, it is not usually necessary to deal with the operating system directly.

There is one exception: all software is written to match a specific operating system. Any new software you buy has to match the operating system you already have on your machine. If, for example, you have a spreadsheet that works with (the technical term is **runs under**) the popular Windows system, then buying software written for a different system such as Unix is a waste of time and money. It will not work. Find out which operating system your computer uses, and make sure that new software is compatible.

Ease of use

Operating systems work on two levels. The most visible level is the **user interface** which you use to work with your machine.

It determines the 'look and feel' of your computer, and also how easily you can get work done.

Some operating systems use pictures on the screen to show what your options are. These are known as GUIs (Graphical User Interfaces) and are designed to be as easy to use as possible. Software that works with GUIs has on-screen 'buttons' and other controls. You use these with a mouse that is plugged into the computer – a palm-sized plastic object that sits next to your keyboard and controls a movable pointer or cursor on the screen. You select different options by clicking with the mouse. This means moving the pointer over a 'button' on the screen, and then pressing one of the two real buttons on the mouse to select it.

Most GUIs also include a drag-and-drop facility. To move a sentence or paragraph in a document you can simply highlight it with the mouse then drag and drop it by holding one of the buttons down, moving the pointer to a new location and releasing the button. The sentence disappears from the old location and appears in the new one. This makes editing very quick and easy. Drag-and-drop features are used in all kinds of software.

Older operating systems work on a text-only basis known as a command-line interface. To work with one of these older systems you have to learn a set of commands, such as COPY, which moves information from one place to another, and DIR which lists all the information on your hard disk. To use these commands you type them on the keyboard, hit the RETURN key and the computer responds to your request. Editing tends to be much slower with this kind of operating system.

Text-only systems date from a time when computers were much less powerful, and text was all they could handle. This is no longer true today and it is likely that by the end of the 1990s text-only systems will be all but obsolete. However, they are still preferred for some kinds of work. They give you more control and have the advantage of working with cheaper and less powerful hardware.

The less visible level of an operating system is the system interface – a complex set of connections to the hardware. This standardises the way the hardware works. This part of the operating system is completely hidden from users.

Some operating systems let your computer do more than one thing at a time. You can start off a long calculation, compose a fax, send it, write a letter, print it out and log a phone call, all while the computer continues with the calculation 'in the background'. This useful ability is known as pre-emptive multitasking (usually shortened to multitasking.)

A multitasking operating system is – nominally – more reliable. Each task is managed so that it works independently of the others. If the task runs into problems or attempts something impossible, the computer as a whole does not hang or crash. The problem task can be stopped while the others carry on regardless.

A simpler version of multitasking is known as task-switching. This allows you to switch between different applications quickly and easily and can be very useful. You can be working on a letter, decide you need to check an address in your information manager, switch to it quickly, and then come back to the letter which remains exactly as you left it. Without task-switching you would have to unload the word-processing software, load in the information manager (time-consuming even on a fast machine), unload the organiser, load in the word processor and return to your place.

Older operating systems work on a strict one-job-at-a-time basis. The best they can manage is a feature called **print spooling**. This means you can print a letter without having to wait for the printer to finish – the printing itself continues in the background while you get on with other work. This feature is usually part of the software, rather than of the operating system.

Like other software, operating systems evolve and go through different versions. Some are radically different from their predecessors; for example, Windows version 1 and Windows version 3 are completely different operating systems. Others offer much smaller changes. It is important when looking at operating systems to include the version number, as the differences between versions can sometimes cause problems.

Only a handful of operating systems are available today. The ones you are likely to come across include:

MS-DOS (IBM PC)

MS-DOS (Microsoft Disk Operating System) is the original PC operating system. It is sold by Microsoft, the world's leading PC software company. MS–DOS was devised in the late 1970s but has maintained its position because so many people use it. MS–DOS (often shortened to DOS) is a command–line system. It can only do one thing at a time.

In terms of modern computing, MS–DOS is a throwback to the age of the dinosaurs. It can be something of a nightmare for beginners as it does not appear user-friendly or accommodating. However, it is the lowest common denominator between different PC machines. A program written to use MS–DOS on a very early PC will work on an up-to-date model.

The one great advantage of DOS is that it is simple and unfussy. It will work on the oldest and least impressive hardware and will place minimal demands on it. In general, however, it is ham-fisted and obstructive. It was designed when computers were basic and slow, and users had to be forced to work them in a way that suited the computer, rather than the user. Graphics are minimal and crude and the software can seem clumsy when compared with later examples that use a more modern operating system.

MS–DOS is currently up to version 6.2. (Windows 95 includes version 7 of DOS, but unlike DOS 6.2 this is not available as a separate product, and is kept well hidden from most users.) Version 6.0, which is still on sale, is best avoided, as it can cause problems with some hard disk systems. Version 5 is still sold by some unscrupulous dealers; avoid this too. The latest version includes some useful new features that can make life slightly easier for users.

Windows (IBM PC)

Like MS–DOS, Windows was created by Microsoft, although it is based on earlier products from Apple and Xerox. It covers a range of operating systems.

The name derives from the way in which the screen can be split up into areas or 'windows' each of which has a frame. Each window can be moved, opened, closed and resized without affecting the others. This makes it possible to have a word processor in one window and a spreadsheet in another. To swap between them you move the mouse pointer to the window you want to work with, click on it once and it becomes active.

Current versions are Windows 3.1, 3.11 and Windows 95. Windows 3.1 and 3.11 (which are known together as legacy Windows or Windows 3.1x) are not quite true operating systems, because they use MS-DOS as a system interface. Windows exists on top of MS-DOS to make it easier to use and more appealing visually. A corollary of this is that if you want to use Windows software, you will need to install a copy of MS-DOS as well. The two are often sold together when you buy your computer.

Windows version 3.11 is designed for use on a multi-user network, although it includes some useful extra features even when used on a single PC. It is sometimes known as Windows for Workgroups (WfWG). Windows 3.1, however, is a single-computer operating system. Both systems offer task-switching and very limited multitasking.

Windows 95 is a total rewrite of the Windows system that attempts to bring it up to date. It includes all kinds of useful extras such as built-in Internet support, improved information handling, proper multitasking for Windows 95-compatible

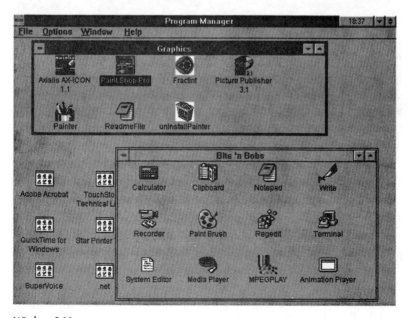

Windows 3.11

software and overhauled screen layout designs. Windows 95 is intended to be much easier to use. From a technical point of view, DOS has been hidden away even further, and Windows 95 can be used to work with applications written for Windows 3.1x, although with some reduction in effectiveness. It also includes 'Plug and Play' features which make it easier to add new hardware to a PC, although these are still not as developed as they could be.

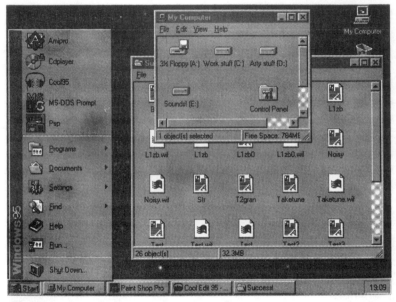

Windows 95

One big disadvantage of Windows 95 is that it demands a much more powerful machine. It can also appear slower and less responsive than earlier versions of Windows, even with fast hardware and plenty of memory. On the other hand, it is much more reliable and easy to use.

If you are using Windows 3.1x and are happy with your current software then there is very little reason to upgrade to Windows 95. You may find you lose some features and your computer will appear to work more slowly, and unless there is a compelling reason to change this is very much a case of not fixing something that is not broken.

On the other hand, new PCs are now supplied with Windows 95 as standard, and providing you choose software that meets your needs there is no reason to complain about this. For most users, most of the time, the difference between this and the older version of Windows is much less than the difference between various examples of application software. The latter will have much more of an effect on your computer's ease of use and speed than the former.

Windows NT (Apple, IBM and others)

NT (New Technology) is the professional version of Windows. It is available on a range of computers, and is designed to be more reliable than standard Windows. It is also much more demanding on hardware – you will need at least 16Mb to run NT comfortably on a PC system. Although at first glance NT looks like standard Windows, internally it works rather differently. It offers extras such as improved security, support for networks and full multitasking. It is also much more expensive.

NT becomes more appealing in a fully professional context, such as a bank or a company with a large network and thus is not recommended for the home or office user with a single computer. Software for Windows NT tends to be aimed at this kind of larger application.

OS/2 and Warp (IBM)

OS/2 was originally intended to be the successor to MS-DOS. It started as a co-operative effort between Microsoft and IBM, but as the two companies became estranged it became IBM's project and Microsoft went on to release Windows.

OS/2 has never caught the imagination of the market in the way that Windows has and sales have been poor. However, the latest version, called Warp, has taken advantage of the fact that Windows 95 is at least 18 months late. Like Windows 95 it offers true multitasking, but it can also multitask Windows 3.1 software, something that Windows 95 can't do.

Opinions of Warp are mixed. The consensus seems to be that when it works it is very good indeed, but getting it to work can be a headache.

211

Some high street retailers are supplying machines with Warp instead of Windows. In theory, Warp should run all Windows 3.1 and MS-DOS software unchanged. In practice, this seems to depend on which hardware is being used.

Use Warp only if you know that the software you want is not available on any other system. IBM seems to have tacitly admitted defeat in its war with Microsoft and at the time of writing, in spite of OS/2's technical advantages its future seems uncertain.

Unix (all computers)

Unix is widely considered (with reason) to be a computer professional's operating system, and hence something of a challenge for non-technical users. Unix is a command-line system and much of its notoriety stems from the way in which command names seem to be obscure and confusing. Fortunately, a graphical extension called X-Windows is available which works rather like Windows or the Macintosh Operating System. Unix is always fully multitasking.

Although Unix is used mainly on powerful machines in large companies, on smaller machines it tends to be the preserve of the hobbyist. A free version, Linux, is particularly popular and is available as freeware. Consultants may recommend it for certain applications, as at best it can be much more powerful and reliable than Windows, and perhaps even Windows NT. Not recommended for beginners.

System 7 and Mac O/S (Apple)

Apple machines have their own Apple-designed operating system, which is currently known as System 7.5. This is a standard Windows-like task-switching system. It is widely considered to be slightly easier to use than Microsoft's Windows and possibly also slightly more reliable.

The latest Apple machines are supplied with Mac O/S (Mac Operating System) which is System 7.5 under another name. There are a few very minor modifications which make it suitable for third-party use, now that Apple has started licensing its products to other manufacturers.

In 1996 a new version of the operating system, known variously as System 8 and Copland, will be made available. This will offer full multitasking, improve on a number of other features and will work more efficiently with the latest Apple PowerMac computers.

OpenDoc

OpenDoc is a new operating system standard that works in a different way from previous products. Software for OpenDoc is sold in the form of tools for specific simple tasks. OpenDoc allows these to be used together. Its big advantage is that software created this way is smaller, more efficient and uses computer resources much more effectively. It also matches users' needs more precisely. Current software on all computers tends to be huge and unwieldy, with many features remaining ignored or undiscovered. OpenDoc will solve this problem by allowing users to create software 'tool-kits' to match their individual needs. Unfortunately, towards the end of 1995 the OpenDoc initiative seemed to founder slightly, and it is now not clear when or if OpenDoc software will become available to the public in its full form.

THE IBM PC

WHEN YOU start looking at different computer makes and models, you will find that by far the most readily available and widely publicised brand of computer on the market today is the IBM-compatible PC.

PC stands for 'Personal Computer'. In this context it means a computer that is designed to be used by one person at a time and to fit conveniently on a desk. This can apply to any small computer but in practice the letters 'PC' have become synonymous with IBM-compatible machines.

IBM-compatibles are manufactured from standard parts manufactured in the United States and South-East Asia. Smaller dealers simply assemble these to order. Larger manufacturers, notably IBM, Dell, Compaq and Gateway, put together their machines from parts they have designed and manufactured themselves.

Whatever their origin, all PCs conform to the same design standard originally defined by IBM (International Business Machines). In practical terms this means that any software that is 'written for a PC' will work on any of these machines. It also means that it is easy to exchange information between machines.

Over the years the IBM PC standard has undergone a number of revisions. Newer models can do everything that the older models could and usually much more quickly. Each aspect of the design has been refined and updated, and this process continues today. The full range of machines is still available, although the older models can only be bought second-hand.

Instead of brand names, PCs are distinguished by the model of computer chip at their heart. This master chip (also known as the processor or central processing unit (CPU)) is rather like the engine in a car – it is the main component that does most of the work. All the other parts of a computer exist to get information into and out of this chip.

Some computer chips work faster than others. A chip's speed is quoted in MHz – millions of cycles a second. This means that a chip that runs at 10MHz will run just over twice as fast as the same model of chip that runs at 5MHz. Unfortunately, this does not mean that the computer will work twice as fast – the speed of a computer system as a whole depends on a number of other factors. However, the processor speed does give a basic indication of a computer's power.

Here is a guide to the PCs you will see advertised, together with star ratings for *cost* (more stars means lower cost), *performance* (more stars means a faster computer) and *value for money* (more stars means a better price/performance ratio).

8088/8086 (4.77MHz, 10MHz)

Cost: ★★★★★
Performance: ★
Value for money: ★★
Suggested applications: Very simple word processing, accountancy and (at a push) spreadsheet and database work.
Pros: Very, very low cost (typically £75 or less).
Cons: Slow, dated and not powerful enough for anything other than the simplest and most undemanding tasks. Getting new software and spare parts for these machines is likely to be a problem.
Expansion: ISA bus slots – on some machines only.
Floppy disks: 5.25-inch as standard, 360K 3.5-inch disks available occasionally.
Hard disks: Usually no more than around 30Mb if fitted at all.
Typical memory supplied: 640K maximum.

These first-generation machines appeared in the mid-1980s and are hopelessly outdated in modern terms. They are worth considering for serious work only if you are working to the tightest of tight budgets and need a computer for very simple tasks such as writing letters and basic bookkeeping. They are suitable for those who want to dabble and learn the basics without a large outlay. You may sometimes see them advertised as 'PC–XT' compatibles. They cannot run Windows software.

80286 (6MHz – 20MHz) (286)

Cost: ★★★★
Performance: ★
Value for money: ★★
Suggested applications: Word processing and office work.
Pros: Reasonable computer power at a modest price (£200 or less).
Cons: Dated and not able to cope with the latest software. Difficult to upgrade to a full modern specification.
Expansion: ISA bus. (A few Compaq and IBM machines may offer EISA and/or MCA bus expansion as well.)
Floppy disks: 5.25-inch as standard, although most machines can easily be upgraded to 3.5-inch disks.
Hard disks: Sometimes standard, not usually more than 120Mb.
Typical memory supplied: Usually 1Mb, occasionally 2Mb.
These are the oldest machines that can be used to do useful work in an office. Although much slower than more recent models, they can handle word processing, spreadsheet calculations and office accounts and could serve the needs of the sole trader and small business user on a very tight budget. Sometimes known as 'PC-AT' compatibles, while the chips themselves are known as '286' chips. (This also applies to other chips in the series – thus 386 and 486 are short for 80386 and 80486.) Their main drawback is the lack of available software. These machines are able to run the older version of Windows, but they do so very slowly and with important technical limitations, and therefore cannot be recommended for this purpose. Only worth considering if appropriate software is available with the computer when it is bought.

80386SX & DX (16MHz – 40MHz) (386)

Cost: ★★★
Performance: ★★
Value for money: ★★
Suggested applications: Suitable for business use if not using Windows 95.
Pros: Very sluggish compared to recent machines.
Cons: Light office work. Suitable (if slow) for legacy Windows applications. Not suitable for Windows 95.
Expansion: ISA bus slots.
Floppy disks: SX: Equal likelihood of 5.25-inch and 3.5-inch disks. DX: Usually 3.5-inch 720K, although sometimes 3.5-inch 1.44Mb disks are standard.
Hard disk: SX: Often, but not always, standard; usually between 100Mb and 200Mb. DX: Usually standard, between 120Mb and 340Mb.
Typical memory supplied: SX: 1Mb, 2Mb, sometimes 4Mb. DX: Typically 2Mb, sometimes 4Mb or even 8Mb.

These machines were the top line models in the early 1990s. The SX version is significantly slower than the DX and is best avoided. They can be upgraded with an 80387 coprocessor chip to speed up arithmetical calculations, and can run older Windows 3.1x software, but not software written for Windows 95. Technologically, these machines are obsolete and it is impossible to upgrade them. They are not recommended unless they suit a buyer's needs 'as seen' with all appropriate software included.

80486SX & SX2 (25MHz – 66MHz)

Cost: ★★★
Performance: ★★
Value for money: ★★★
Suggested applications: Light office work. Can work with older Windows software and Windows 95.
Pros: Good value for simple office tasks.
Cons: Very slow at arithmetical work (such as spreadsheets).
Expansion: ISA and VLB slots.
Floppy disks: 3.5-inch 1.44Mb standard.

Hard disk: Standard between 250Mb and 540Mb.

Typical memory supplied: 4Mb, sometimes 8Mb.

The SX and SX2 are being targeted at the small office user, but DX and DX2 chip machines are much faster at arithmetical work and cost only very slightly more. Unless a dealer can make you a support offer, or include plenty of genuinely useful free software, avoid these models.

80486DX, DX2, DX4, DX5 (33MHz – 150MHz)

Cost: ★★★
Performance: ★★★
Value for money: ★★★★

Suggested applications: Powerful enough for everyday applications. Can work with older Windows software and Windows 95.

Pros: The faster models especially are good budget machines with plenty of power.

Cons: A touch sluggish when working with Windows 95 software.

Expansion: ISA and VLB slots. Some machines offer PCI slots.

Floppy disks: 3.5-inch 1.44Mb standard.

Hard disk: Standard, between 250Mb and 540Mb.

Typical memory supplied: 4Mb, sometimes 8Mb.

The DX4/120 and DX5/150 models are faster than a cheap Pentium machine. They offer good value for home and small business users and, although their working life is now limited, they provide reasonable and affordable computing power at a modest price. For Windows 95 use, 16Mb of memory is strongly recommended. As an upgrade this will offer better value for money than a faster processor chip.

Pentium P60 (60MHz)

Cost: ★★
Performance: ★★★
Value for money: ★★

Suggested applications: Average office work.

Pros: Faster than an equivalent 486 processor, especially for work which involves lots of numerical calculations (e.g., working with large spreadsheets).

Cons: Not good value compared to other Pentiums and already obsolete.

Expansion: ISA and PCI slots.

Floppy disks: 3.5-inch 1.44Mb as standard.

Hard disk: Typically 420Mb fitted as standard.

Typical memory supplied: 8Mb, sometimes 16Mb.

The 60MHz and 66MHz Pentiums were introduced at the end of 1994, and have since been made redundant by faster, and in many cases cheaper, Pentium machines. Now only available second-hand, models built around these chips may also suffer from the Pentium bug (see note at the end of this chapter). Not recommended under any circumstances, as other Pentium models offer much better value for money.

Slow Pentiums (75MHz – 100MHz)

Cost: ★★
Performance: ★★★★
Value for money: ★★★★★

Suggested applications: Office and home use and advanced applications such as large spreadsheets, image editing and sound and video work.

Pros: Probably the best price/performance ratio of any PC at the moment and, unlike cheaper models, these are likely to have a reasonable working life.

Cons: None!

Expansion: ISA and PCI bus slots.

Floppy disks: 3.5-inch 1.44Mb as standard.

Hard disk: 540Mb, up to 1Gb (SCSI).

Typical memory supplied: 8Mb, sometimes 16Mb.

These models, and especially the middle-of-the-range P90, are fast enough to work with all the latest Windows 95 software, and are now being sold for a very reasonable price. For most applications, the difference between the P75, P90 and P100 is not nearly as significant as the difference between a machine with 8Mb of memory and one with 16Mb. A 16Mb P90 provides perhaps the ideal combination for home and office use, and offers a good level of performance and working life.

Fast Pentiums (120MHz – 200MHz)

Cost: ★
Performance: ★★★★★
Value for money: ★★
Suggested applications: Demanding work such as unusually large spreadsheets, sound and video editing, CAD, image manipulation and professional DTP.
Pros: Very fast indeed.
Cons: Relatively expensive.
Expansion: ISA and PCI bus slots.
Floppy disks: 3.5-inch 1.44Mb as standard.
Hard disk: 540Mb, up to 1Gb (SCSI).
Typical memory supplied: 8Mb, 16Mb, sometimes 32Mb.
These machines are far too powerful and expensive for everyday office use, and should be considered only for very heavy-duty work. Suitable for very high-powered applications such as network servers, CAD, computer animations and video conferencing.

P6 now called Pentium Pro (150MHz upwards)

Cost: ★
Performance: ★★★★★
Value for money: ★★
Suggested applications: Very demanding professional computing tasks. Ideally suited for use with Windows NT. Not ideal for Windows 95.
Pros: Very, very fast indeed.
Cons: A quirk in the design makes these models poor value for Windows 95 users.
Expansion: ISA and fast PCI.
Floppy disks: 3.5-inch 1.44 Mb as standard.
Hard disk: 1Gb upwards.
Typical memory supplied: 8Mb to 32Mb.
The Pentium Pro is aimed at the serious business user with a limitless budget who demands plenty of extra computing power. Because of a design flaw, when used with Windows 95 they may actually be slower – or at least not significantly faster – than a

much cheaper Pentium machine. Not recommended for everyday business use.

Multiprocessor systems (Pentium and Pentium Pro)

Cost: ★
Performance: ★★★★
Value for money: ★
Suggested applications: Ideal for Windows NT users. Not recommended for everyday office work.
Pros: Can be even faster than a single Pentium Pro system.
Cons: Very, very expensive indeed.
Expansion: ISA and fast PCI.
Floppy disks: 3.5-inch 1.44Mb as standard.
Hard disk: 750Mb upwards.
Typical memory supplied: 8Mb to 64Mb.

Multiprocessor systems divide up the workload between more than one processor chip inside the same box. In theory, adding more chips means work gets done more quickly. In practice, technical restrictions make the speed gains much lower than might be expected. Software has to be specially written to use the extra power of multiprocessor systems. Currently most software isn't, although users of Windows NT will be able to make some use of the improved speed these models offer. These models are still rare, and are not recommended for beginners. They are included here for completeness.

THE PENTIUM BUG

In computer-speak, a 'bug' is a design flaw and, whether found in hardware or software, can cause reliability and/or accuracy problems. Bugs cause your computer to stop working or give you the wrong answer to a calculation.

Early versions of the Pentium processor (specifically those produced before February 1995) included a bug which gave the wrong result for certain long-division calculations.

For most users this bug is more of an irritation than a major worry. The error introduced is slight – of the order of a few pence in a calculation working with tens of thousands of pounds – and happens only with a small range of numbers. For engineering, medical and other professional applications the chip should be replaced. This is a free service from Intel.

If you have an older machine, you can check for the bug by trying out the following calculation using the calculator utility supplied with the Windows operating system. All the digits must be entered exactly as shown -

4195835 / 3145727 × 3145727 – 4195835

If the result is not zero your machine has the bug. However, this test is not quite 100 per cent reliable, and to be sure you should use a simple test program called CPUIDF.EXE which is available directly from Intel. If you have a modem you can also obtain the program directly from Intel's bulletin board on 01793 432955. For more information call Intel's technical support line on 01793 431144.

THE APPLE MACINTOSH

THE APPLE Macintosh (the 'Mac') computer has a long and colourful history. Unlike the IBM PC, which has always been very much a corporate design, the Apple Mac was conceived as an attempt to make a computer that was easy to use and appealing to non-business people.

Apple machines are the computer of choice for many artists, graphic designers and publishing houses. They are less popular with businesses, which tend to choose the more widely used IBM PC-compatible machines.

The Apple Mac offers a number of important advantages for absolute beginners. Firstly, it is undoubtedly easier to use and set up. Upgrading a PC is usually best left to a specialist, but almost anyone can upgrade a Mac. Older PCs need to be set up after some new hardware has been installed, but a Mac will often accept the upgrade and work out what needs to be changed for itself. This can save time and temper in a professional setting, and can also help build confidence among users.

All modern Macs include networking facilities as standard. It is possible to set up a simple network – which can share information among users and make the best use of common resources such as printers – for little more than the cost of a few cables. A simple electronic mail facility, called QuickMail, is also available, and this can be used to exchange messages between different computers on one site.

All Macs are built to a high standard, whereas PCs can vary greatly in build quality and reliability. The Mac looks good and works well.

After the range became established, Apple split the product line into two areas. Domestic Macs are aimed at home users and professionals working at home. Professional Macs are targeted at publishing houses and professionals who need power and can afford to pay for it. Domestic models tend to cost roughly as much as an equivalent PC. Professional models are usually significantly more expensive.

At the top end of the market many Apple Macs are fitted with extras which speed up certain kinds of work. These specialised upgrades have no equivalent in the PC world, and so it is difficult to compare the two kinds of computer on a like-for-like basis. These top-level Macs are recommended for computer-intensive work such as image manipulation, photo-retouching and professional magazine publishing.

The best way to decide whether or not a Mac system is for you is suitable to find a local Apple dealer – many advertise in *Yellow Pages* or in local directories – and try out a system for yourself. Explain your needs to the dealer, try out some relevant software and then do the same with a similarly priced PC system.

Over the decade or so that the Mac has been available, Apple has released a regular stream of new product announcements and name changes. A complete list would take up many pages, so a summary is presented here.

Mac Classic series – Classic, Colour Classic, 128, 512, SE, SE/30 and Plus

These are the original Macs in the original all-in-one case. Memory is minimal – a mere 128K in the '128' version – and no more than 4Mb in the SE/30. Hard disks are either small or absent. These models are suitable for word processing, but otherwise belong in the 'vintage' category. There are no internal expansion slots.

Mac II range – Mac II, IIx, IIcx, IIci, IIsi, IIvi and IIvx and IIfx

These were powerful machines in their day, especially the IIfx, but are now somewhat dated. They were aimed at professional users.

Memory was expandable up to 32Mb in some cases and hard disks are standard. NuBus slots were included to allow for expansion.

Mac LC range – LC I, II & III, LC460, LC475, LC520 and LC630

These are all domestic Macs. The LC was roughly equivalent to a Classic, and is now very dated. The LC II is only slightly more powerful. The others are all very adequate second-hand machines and are suitable for light business use. The 630 can be fitted with a TV tuner card and NICAM stereo decoder system.

Performa range – Performa 630, 5200, 5300, 6200

These are the latest generation of domestic Macs, and all except the 630 offer Power PC performance at a reasonable price. The 5200 and 5300 are single-box models that contain the computer and colour monitor in a single case, which helps reduce unsightly cabling. The Performas are designed very much as home entertainment centres, and CD-ROM drives, TV tuner cards (which can also grab 'stills' from TV programmes) and NICAM stereo decoders are either available as options or included in the basic price.

Quadra range – Centris 610, 650, 650AV, Quadra 605, 610, 650, 700, 800, 840AV, 900 and 950

These were aimed at professional users and were the top of the line until the PowerMac models were introduced in 1994. Any of these, especially the more powerful models (with a higher model number), are more than adequate for business use. The AV models include extra hardware to record and playback sound at CD quality.

Original PowerMac range – 6100, 7100, 8100

These machines were the first to use the new and more powerful PowerPC chip, and are significantly faster than older Macs. To be used at their best they need special 'native mode' software. PowerMacs can run software written for older Macs, but they do this rather slowly. These models, especially the still-competitive 8100, come the NuBus expansion slots, and are worth considering on the second-hand market.

Newer PowerMac range – 7200, 7500, 7600, 8200, 8500, 9500

The latest PowerMacs are aimed squarely at professional users. They are built around either the PowerPC 601 or the faster 604 chips, which are second-generation improved versions of the PowerPC 603 used in the first PowerMacs. Unlike earlier Macs they have built-in PCI slots, which are faster than NuBus slots and can take a wider range of hardware options. They are very fast but relatively expensive.

PowerMac clones

Apple is now licensing its technology to other manufacturers, which means that for the first time Apple-like computers are available from companies other than Apple. Power Computing with its Power 120 model is the most prominent manufacturer of Mac clones, although other companies may be working on models. This is a very fast-moving part of the market, and for the most up-to-date information it is a good idea to read the Apple monthlies. For more details, see the Apple section in Appendix XI.

Powerbook 100 series – 100, 140, 145, 145b, 150, 160, 165, 165c, 170, 180, 180c, 190 and 190cs

These are portable Macs, and are quite light enough to be used as notebooks. Specifications vary. The original 100 is now obsolete. The others are still viable as portable machines and the 190 is still being sold today. Models with the 'c' suffix include a colour screen.

Powerbook Duo series – 210, 230, 250, 270c, 280 and 280c

These are docking station computers. Unlike the other models they do not include a floppy disk drive or a printer connection, although an Apple network socket is provided. They are lighter and easier to carry around than the other Powerbooks, and can be used as normal desktops if connected to the docking station. This allows a normal keyboard, a floppy disk drive and a printer to be connected. (For more details on docking stations see Appendix VII.)

Powerbook 500 series – 520, 520c, 540 and 540c

These are Powerbooks with the same speed and power as the old Quadra range (in many ways they are simply portable versions of these). They have a PDS slot and can be upgraded to the latest PowerPC system boards. Instead of the usual trackball, the 500 series uses a track pad system which responds to finger pressure.

Powerbook Power PC series – 5300 and 5300c

These latest Powerbooks use the PowerPC chip, and are as fast as some of the PowerPC desktop models. They are far too powerful for the kind of simple word processing and contact management for which most notebooks are used. On the other hand, these machines make it possible to continue with almost any kind of work away from the office, including DTP and CAD. However, like other portables they are not cheap.

Apple extras

Some extras are specific to Apple machines. The most interesting is the Quicktake camera. This is a film-less camera which stores images in computer memory that can then be transferred to any Mac for further processing.

Many professional users use a special kind of data cartridge known as a Syquest drive. This is like a standard hard disk drive, except that it uses a removable cartridge instead of a fixed drive. These cartridges are used instead of floppy disks for work that needs a high volume of data, such as publishing and colour origination. Many printing bureaux accept these cartridges. The common sizes are 44Mb and 88Mb, though 200Mb are also becoming standard. They are also a good choice as a backup medium.

OTHER BRANDS OF COMPUTER

IN TERMS of sales alone, IBM-compatibles and the various versions of the Apple Macintosh account for almost all of the market. There are other brands, however, most of which date back to the early 1980s when the computer market was split between machines that were used for serious work and those that were used for games and entertainment. Although most of these are no longer available new, they are still widely available on the second-hand market.

The main disadvantage of these brands is a lack of service and support, and the fact that they have become increasingly marginalised as the home-computer market has matured. IBM-compatibles and Apple Macs are an industry standard and information and software are all widely available. They therefore cannot be recommended except perhaps for someone who would like to dabble with computers without making a huge investment.

Acorn Archimedes

This is the only machine in this group still on sale today. Acorn originally designed the BBC computer, which was a popular choice for schools and colleges in the early 1980s. To some extent Acorn has kept its grip on this part of the market with its latest machines which are still the standard in primary schools. In secondary schools the trend is now towards PC models and Apple Macs, as these are seen as providing better work-related experience.

It is something of an indictment of the computer trade that Acorn computers have not been more successful. Their software and operating system is at least two or three years ahead of anything the PC market can offer. Unfortunately Acorn does not have the marketing power to take on the PC market, and these machines have remained stuck in their educational niche.

The current top-end product is the RiscPC computer. Older models, such as the A3000 range, are still available. It is possible to buy a plug-in card for these machines that allows them to run PC software in parallel with any other work you are doing on the main machine. Unfortunately this card won't work with PC hardware – it is a software only option.

Acorn computers are worth considering because they tend to be easier to use than the industry leaders. A wide range of software is available, some of it aimed at business users. The option of running PC software is a definite advantage. In general the Acorn is ideal for home and family use, perhaps even as a second computer for use by the children.

With the increasing inroads of the industry leaders into its traditional educational market, Acorn took the bold step at the beginning of 1996 of announcing that it plans to become an Apple clone maker. What this implies for the future of its own products remains uncertain at the time of writing.

For more information look out for *Acorn Archimedes World*, which is perhaps the best all-round Acorn monthly.

Atari

The Atari ST series was originally designed as a games machine, but found favour in the professional music market, largely as a result of the chance inclusion of the music industry-standard MIDI control system.

The Atari range never lived up to its potential as a business machine. The early games-oriented machines had a clunky, rubbery keyboard which was integrated with the main system unit, and this made them unappealing to anyone who needed to do a lot of typing. The floppy disk drives had to be bought separately and were housed outside the main system unit. This often led to a tangle of wires.

The models that are worth serious consideration for business use are the Mega ST and Mega STE ranges. Both have a more usable detached external keyboard and come with a built-in floppy disk. Hard disk drives are available as an extra. One of the best features of the Atari range was the excellent black and white monitor, which is more than adequate for prolonged use and matches or even betters some of the monitors available today.

In terms of software, Write On! and First Word Plus are good choices for word-processing applications, while Calamus offers powerful DTP features as well as simple word-processor style editing features. First Word Plus is adequate for light-duty work, but does not have any of the features needed for professional use.

Other applications are not widely available. Although spreadsheets and communications packages do exist, they can be hard to find. Most Atari machines are sold second-hand with large collections of games or music software. To find an Atari machine for serious use it is best to look in some of the mainstream computer magazines and other Atari-specific journals.

For further information on recent developments look out for *ST Format* magazine, by far the best source of Atari news and information. It is published by Future Publishing and like many of their titles is aimed at younger readers.

Amiga

The Amiga started life as another games machine. It found favour with some programmers, but on the whole was more of a leisure than a business computer. For all this it had some impressive features, and in some ways was more advanced than comparable computers at the time.

Commodore Business Machines who marketed the Amiga foundered in 1994. However, in spring 1995, Escom, a high-street retailer and PC manufacturer, bought the rights to the Amiga range. Since then Escom has been less than aggressive about marketing and developing the Amiga range, preferring instead to concentrate on selling PCs. Although Amigas are still officially available, it now seems certain that this particular line has either come to the end of its working life or will do so very shortly. More information is available in *Amiga Format* magazine.

Amstrad Word Processor Range

These machines, which are known as the PCW range were very popular when they were released in the mid-1980s. Combining basic word-processing software with a keyboard, monitor, disk drives and printer, they were the ideal all-in-one solution for anyone who wanted to write letters but did not have the expertise to take on a complete computer system. However, they are true computers rather than word processors and can handle a range of applications beyond simple word processing.

The technology used in the PCW range is more typical of the 1970s than the 1980s and thus they are very slow. Print quality tends to be poor, although it is possible to connect a more modern bubble-jet printer in place of the dot-matrix or daisy-wheel originals. The software is based on the CP/M operating system which is an early ancestor of MS-DOS. Locoscript is the word-processing software. A version of this is available for the PC, so adventurous PCW users can make a relatively painless transition to a much faster system.

The biggest problem with the PCW range is the non-standard floppy disk format used on earlier models. These use 3-inch disks rather than the more usual 3.5-inch variety. Supplies of these disks are now drying up, but a number of companies offer a 3.5-inch disk upgrade option which allows normal disks to be used. Another disadvantage is price: a PCW system may well prove more expensive than an equivalent vintage PC.

Existing PCW users planning to upgrade should be wary of 'easy upgrades' to PC systems. Although these offer a relatively painless way to get PC power while maintaining a familiar PCW style approach, some of these are being sold at hugely inflated prices. When considering one of these systems be sure to shop around first and see if the equivalent is available at a much more reasonable price.

For more information on the PCW range, look out for *PCW Plus* magazine.

Amstrad PCs

In the mid-1980s Amstrad released a range of PC-compatibles which created their own mini-standard at the lower end of the market. Much of this was due to marketing – these were the first machines that were widely available in the high street. Technically they were simply cheap IBM-compatible machines.

The 1512 and the 1640 are now very much in the 'vintage' category. Many people still use them for word processing and simple tasks. They cannot run modern software or easily be upgraded. But they were popular in their time and are widely available on the second-hand market. Although limited and slow, they are suitable for light use and are a good choice if you need a computer but have a tiny budget. If possible choose a model with a hard disk.

PORTABLE COMPUTERS

A GOOD option for the business user is a powerful expensive computer at work and a relatively cheap portable machine for use everywhere else. It is rare that a portable can take the place of a proper office system, as the small screen and limited battery life mean that its uses are restricted in a practical context. But for light use – letters, invoices, faxes and so on – a cheap portable can be ideal. Expensive portables, which include extras such as a printer, a pair of speakers and a CD-ROM within the case, are an excellent choice for making presentations. Most portables can be hooked up to an external display, which means it is possible to prepare a presentation at home or even on the road, and then present it on location.

Portables are becoming more and more popular. Battery technology is improving all the time, and as batteries get smaller and lighter portables will replace desktop machines. Some of the most exciting developments will be in the field of on-line services. It is now possible to buy modems that work with the cellular phone network, and this means that users can send and receive e-mail messages away from their base of operations. This is likely to transform the way that people communicate with each other.

For now, portable computing is recommended for anyone who needs to be away from his or her base, be it home or office, while maintaining access to records and other information stored back at base. It is also recommended for users who find existing monitor designs difficult to work with. Portables use a different display system that does not flicker in the same way, and some users find this easier.

Portables come in a variety of shapes and sizes. The larger machines are now dated and almost obsolete; newer models are getting smaller and lighter each year. Within the portable family you will find the following kinds of machine:

'Luggables'

Like all portables this includes a computer, a screen and a keyboard all in one case. On these models the keyboard clips down on to the base unit to create a box the size and often the weight of a pilot's briefcase.

These machines are too heavy to be carried long distances and much too large to be used in trains or on planes, but they can easily be taken home after a day's work or placed on a desk in a client's office. Unlike 'true' portables they need to be plugged into the mains supply to work – batteries are not only not included, but not an option.

There are very few luggable computers available these days and their only advantage over a desktop machine is the absence of wires. Anyone looking for a portable can find a similarly specified but much more manageable machine for less money.

Portables

'True' portables are still unwieldy, although they can be carried quite a distance. They tend to be large and bulky, and like luggables are rapidly being superseded by more modern designs. Because many of these models are now obsolete they cannot be expanded in the way that more modern machines can. Battery life is poor and like luggables they are better suited for desk work rather than for use on trains and planes. They do have batteries, however, so in theory can be used anywhere.

Notebooks

Notebook machines are a much more manageable size and weight. They are usually more or less A4 size, but offer features which are similar to those found in desktop machines. All-in-one models which include extras such as printers, modems and CD-ROM drives within the one case, are now available, although it is doubtful whether these are light enough to be easily carried a long way. Modern notebooks are expandable using the PCMCIA system and this allows tiny extras such as modems and soundcards – some of which are literally credit card size – to be plugged into the case. Notebooks have become the portable standard since the early 1990s.

Sub-notebooks

These are even smaller versions of the standard notebook design. Sub-notebooks are an excellent choice for a general-purpose information manager and portable word-processing tool. They can be used for most of the tasks a desktop computer can, but they are light enough to carry around with ease.

Electronic organisers and palmtop computers

At the bottom end of the market is the electronic organiser. This is an electronic version of the ring-bound paper diary/address book/notebook that was popular in the 1980s. Although slow compared with a well-specified desktop machine, electronic organisers can be useful tools. Larger electronic organisers are often known as palmtops. These are very simple, very cheap, full-function PCs in a handheld case. Most offer the following features:

An electronic notepad or word processor This can be used to store notes and jottings or as a letter-writing tool. The options available tend to be very basic, however, and writing a long piece which appears in a tiny window can be frustrating for anyone used to a larger display area.

An electronic address book and phone number database This works exactly likes its paper counterpart, except that entries can be amended more easily. One useful feature available on some organisers is an auto-dialler. By holding the organiser close to the mouthpiece, it can simulate dialling tones.

An electronic diary Appointments can be scheduled into the organiser and it can be programmed to produce an audible reminder before the event itself.

A clock Most organisers include a world time-zone facility.

A few organisers also offer useful additional features such as a calculator, currency conversion keys and unit conversion options.

Most organisers can be linked to a desktop computer and information transferred between the two. This is an important facility – it means you can keep safety copies of your contacts on your main machine in case the organiser is lost or stolen.

All electronic organisers suffer from similar drawbacks: the keyboards and display windows are usually too small to be convenient. Most manufacturers resort to miniaturised keys in an attempt to work around this. Anyone used to typing on a full-sized keyboard may find it very hard to adapt.

In spite of this, electronic organisers can be a useful option if you cannot afford a full portable or if you need a handy portable address book and notepad.

Personal Digital Assistant

The Personal Digital Assistant (PDA) is the next generation of portable computer products. The technology is in its infancy, and repeated customer surveys and magazine tests have shown that none of the current models are as useful or as usable as conventional organisers. As the technologies mature, however, it is likely that these will be the machines of the future.

PDAs offer the following extras over and above those found in an organiser:

Handwriting recognition The computer can recognise words and phrases 'written' with a stylus on the PDA's message window. The stylus can also be used to draw maps and take notes. Handwriting systems have improved dramatically over the last year or so. The latest version of the Apple Newton in particular has come much closer to fulfilling its potential in this respect.

Many PDAs also include 'intelligent' features that attempt to second guess what you are trying to do. For example, if you write in 'lunch' followed by a person's name, it will call up the diary section, enter a lunch date and perhaps include the other person's telephone number.

Cellular communications

Although on-line services such as the Internet are just starting to become popular, the real revolution will happen when e-mail and other communication systems are freed from their reliance on physical phone lines. Portable modems that use cellular technology to provide an integrated communication system are now available without using telephone lines. However, cellular modems are very expensive and slow compared with their more conventional equivalents. But as the technology develops and systems become cheaper it is very likely that portables will come to replace desktop machines altogether, and that it will be possible to arrange meetings and dinner dates away from the phone, directly from organiser to organiser.

Docking stations

Some portables can be plugged into a larger base unit – a docking station – when used on the desk. This base unit contains extras – expansion slots, an option for a better keyboard and perhaps a better display – which will not fit into a standard portable. The idea is that when 'docked' the whole system becomes a substitute for a proper desktop unit.

Docking stations are expensive compared with standard portables. One of the best examples is Apple's DuoDock series of machines. To keep their weight down these are sold without a floppy disk drive. This is available only as an optional extra.

Buying tips

When buying a notebook you should remember to check with your dealer the level of support and service offered. Will the dealer's service scheme cover you if something goes wrong when you are on the road?

Check what software comes with the portable. A very useful extra is a data exchange program which enables you to transfer

241

information to your main PC. On some machines this will need additional hardware. Other features to check for include:

Weight How easy is it to carry the portable? Is it as portable and light as an organiser, or is it more 'luggable' and unwieldy?

Display quality Try the computer out and look closely at the display. Watch out for mouse pointers that disappear when you move them, and for overall brightness and clarity. Will the display still be visible in bright sunlight? In general TFT (thin film transistor) displays give the best results, but these are very expensive – expect to pay between £500 and £1,000 extra. (These displays are so good that some users fit a screen filter which lowers the viewing angle, so they can do confidential work in public.)

Both colour and monochrome displays are widely available. Most monochrome displays are actually *greyscale* which means that a range of shades is possible, rather than plain black (or blue or green) and white. Colour is a useful extra, but not essential for most work.

How does the mouse work? On portables, mouse pointers come in all shapes and sizes. Some manufacturers supply a standard mouse, although this can prove unwieldy for public use. Avoid the clip-on track ball, which hangs off the keyboard in a rather awkward way. (A trackball is an upside down mouse – you move the screen pointer by wheeling the ball around.) Some clip-on pointers are suitable for right-handed users only. The built-in track ball is more convenient and should be placed in front of the keyboard, at the centre. Best of all perhaps is the trackpoint system, which uses a tiny plastic stub which sits between the G, B and H keys on the keyboard. Although small, this pointer system is very easy to use. Another good choice is the *track pad* – an area which is sensitive to finger pressure. As you slide your finger around the mouse pointer follows.

If you are left-handed, you should also check where the mouse buttons are. On some models they are placed on the right-hand side of the keyboard; on the better designs they are in the centre.

Battery life You can expect a couple of hours of use from nickel cadmium (NiCad) batteries, maybe twice that from NiMH

(Nickel Magnesium Hydride) type batteries. Lithium ion designs are the latest development and promise improved power capacity in a smaller and lighter package.

Check if any spare batteries are included. These can be a useful, if expensive, extra which allow you to keep working for longer without access to a power source. The best portables allow batteries (and other extras) to be 'hot-swapped' – plugged in and out without turning the machine off. International compatibility is also worth watching for – will your portable work directly off the mains supply of another country?

It is advisable to check power-management options and power-down features. Some machines include a very useful 'sleep' mode, which lets you carry on working from exactly where you were when you turned the machine off. Others need to be powered down more deliberately if you want to keep your work.

Power management features range from simple battery meters to optional power saving modes which will temporarily power down a hard disk if it is not used for a set time.

External connectors On some machines a floppy disk drive is an optional and external extra. If you have a connection to a desktop machine, you may not find this is a problem. But if your portable is your only computer you will need some way to get software into it and information out of it. Check if a floppy disk drive is included, and whether or not it is built into the machine.

Check also whether or not you can connect a printer. Some machines, especially those built for docking stations, do not let you do this directly.

On IBM–compatible portables check the number and type of PCMCIA slots. If you need a modem and a soundcard for example, check that the portable has room for these extras. You should also check the available memory. 4Mb is the minimum for an older Windows-compatible machine, while 8Mb is required for Windows 95. If you are using an older model with 2Mb or less then you should ask if an upgrade is possible, and if so how much it will add to the price.

Infra red links The very latest organisers include an IR information transfer system. This makes it easy to exchange information with other organisers and suitably equipped PCs.

On-line services and the Internet

Bulletin board systems (BBSs)

There are hundreds of BBSs in the UK, many of which have a distinct area of interest of their own, ranging from the formal and professional to the extremely strange and disturbing. Some are lively and sociable and may sometimes organise face-to-face social events; to a large extent it depends on the enthusiasm, energy and friendliness of the owner of the board known as the **sysop**. BBSs come in two varieties. The first are run by hobbyists, enthusiasts and computer clubs. These are usually free, although there may be a small annual membership fee (not usually more than £30) for some services. Most hobbyist boards are run on an informal basis. When dialling in for the first time you may be asked to fill in a questionnaire.

The second kind of bulletin board is a strictly commercial venture. These often advertise in computer magazines and usually offer two telephone access numbers. The first puts you through to a section of the BBS where you can see what is available. The second – on an 0891 telephone number or other charge-by-the-minute basis – is used when you want to copy information to your computer. Commercial BBSs do not usually offer anything more than a free bulletin board, and the 0891 access system can make them expensive.

BBS in theory and practice

Bulletin boards are used for playing games, exchanging messages and software. Games are often multi-player and can prove costly in terms of phone bills. Many boards include large public areas which contain shareware and freeware software, as well as other information such as pictures and computer art, sounds and so on. All of these can be accessed via the telephone to your computer, often for free.

Messages are the lifeblood of any board and are organised into conferences, each of which has a topic (computers, football, politics and so on). You may find that you will not be given access to some conferences until you subscribe. Apart from general chatter about topics of the day, you can also use the message facilities to get technical help. Many board users are computer professionals who will sometimes offer advice when they come across a struggling newcomer.

Bulletin boards tend to attract younger, computer-literate, male users and to the more mature user the exchanges can seem inane.

Most boards are connected together in loose networks. These allow messages to be passed between users of different boards – internationally if need be – as well as within the board itself. The most popular network is FidoNet. FidoNet allows you to exchange mail with anyone on another FidoNet board anywhere in the world. But unlike the Internet (see below) mail and messages exchanged this way move slowly. They are transferred between boards at night. It can take a while for a message to get through the system, and you can expect a delay of up to a week before you get a reply.

Some boards also offer an Internet service. Unlike a true electronic mail account, which works almost instantaneously, BBS Internet mail is sent and received at set times – usually once or twice a day. This means it can take a couple of days to get a reply, instead of a couple of hours. But for anyone dabbling with e-mail this is a good opportunity to learn the basics at minimal expense.

To access a bulletin board you will need a piece of software known as a **terminal emulator**. This turns your computer into a dumb keyboard-plus-screen remote window into the BBS computer at the other end of the phone. Terminal emulators are available as shareware from any good shareware source.

Once you are familiar with the basics, you should get hold of an **off-line reader** package (OLR). OLRs let you pull your messages down the phone to your computer in one packet. Once you have disconnected from the line, you can read them and prepare your replies before connecting again to send them back to the board. This is far more cost-effective than the on-line method of reading and replying to messages while actually connected to the board. OLRs are also available as shareware. Off-Line Express and Telix are among the most popular programs.

Finding a BBS

Finding a board can be problematic. Hobbyist boards tend not to advertise and sometimes suffer from limited life-spans. This means that lists have to be updated on a monthly basis. Ideally you want access to a board within your local call area. This can be good socially and also makes for cheaper telephone bills. Calling long distance is possible, but can soon get expensive if you use the board a lot. An up-to-date list of all UK boards — known as the RobList — is carried on many boards. A good way to get hold of it is to join a local board, then explain to the sysop that you are a beginner and would like a copy of the list. *Internet Today* magazine (see Appendix XI) regularly publishes a list of bulletin boards to help you start your search.

International on-line services

These differ from bulletin boards in that they are subscription only (the costs vary) and larger. They offer a similar messaging system to BBSs, but the messages can be a lot livelier and cover a wider range of topics. Almost all services also offer electronic chat, which lets you type messages to other users from your keyboard and read their responses on your monitor. The number of conferences, known as forums, is also much greater. One such service, CompuServe, is known for its huge range of forums, a large proportion of which give you direct access to technical support from software and hardware manufacturers. A number of publications have forums of their own, so that you can make comments and ask questions about magazine features.

Some services also offer electronic shopping. The computer is used as a kind of on-line catalogue, and you can order anything from a bunch of flowers to a new car. Train and flight timetables are also available, and you can check prices, book tickets and arrange flights from your computer.

Financial information is also available. On CompuServe stock market prices are updated with a fifteen-minute delay. A number of brokerage services are also available, so you can track prices and buy and sell almost instantly.

The best way to understand these services is to imagine them as a kind of on-line community. There are meeting areas for various special interest groups, libraries of information contributed by various users, shops, newsagents, travel agents, recreation areas in the form of multi-player games, and a very widely used and active 'instant' postal service.

The drawback of all this is that these services are still fairly expensive. Although CompuServe charges a few pounds a month to cover light use, many of the more potentially profitable services are surcharged. It is easy to run up a huge monthly bill unless you approach the service with discretion. This is also true of other similar services, such as America OnLine (AOL).

The Internet

The Internet originated as a series of experiments designed to create a computer network that could survive nuclear attack.

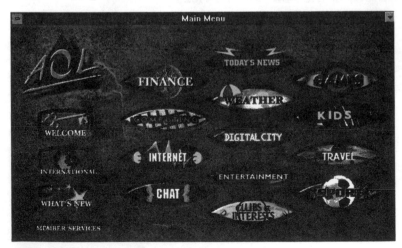

America OnLine is another popular international service

From these rather unpromising beginnings it has evolved into a global computer network linking people in almost every country in the world.

The most useful service available on the Internet is electronic mail. Other networks may have a mail gateway to the outside world but are geared towards exchanging mail internally. With the Internet, however, you can send mail to anyone who has an Internet mail address anywhere, no matter what kind of computer the addressee uses or which system he or she subscribes to.

To access the Internet you need to open an account with an **Internet Service Provider (ISP)**. This allows you to connect your computer directly to the Internet. You can also access all the other Internet services listed in Chapter 6. Providers have points of access (known as PoPs – Points of Presence) dotted around the country. Demon Internet Services, the largest UK provider, has PoPs that cover all of the UK. Others are more localised and often concentrated in the larger cities.

Finding a service provider

The number of providers is growing all the time. Large companies like Microsoft are now considering their own on-line services. The best place to look for an up-to-date list of ISPs is in one of the Internet magazines listed in Appendix XI.

When choosing a provider, it is important to check what kind of software you will be given, and also how good the technical support is. The software should be easy to use, easy to install and offer the full range of services. The most important elements are news (Usenet), e-mail and access to the World Wide Web.

Some providers charge a flat rate per month and allow you to spend as much time on-line as you like. Others charge by the minute or perhaps offer a flat rate up to a certain level of usage and then charge by the minute afterwards. Most take monthly payments, but a handful will ask for a year's payment in advance. Remember that you will also have to pay telephone charges.

Another point to watch is known as the *modem to user ratio*. This is a measure of how easy it is to get a connection when you dial in. A low ratio such as 1:5 means you will probably get through straight away. A high ratio such as 1:30 implies that the provider does not have enough access lines and at peak periods (mainly evenings and weekends) all their lines will be busy.

A handful of providers offer users their own space on the world wide web; often, but not always, for a small extra fee. To use this service you need to know – and perhaps be prepared to pay – someone who understands how to create web pages, or at least be willing to learn how to create them yourself. Fortunately HTML (Hypertext Markup Language – the system used to do this) is reasonable straightforward, even for relative beginners. If you have a service or a product to advertise, or would like to maintain your own pages as a hobby, then web space can be a very useful extra option.

Which? will be launching its own Internet service in the autumn of 1996. As well as providing access to the rest of the Internet, Which? Online will offer on-line versions of the information presented in various Which? magazines, details of campaigns, product recall and safety information, and so on. Subscribers will be able to access further details when they become available.

Cable?

If your home is wired for cable TV, you may be able to avoid the phone charges associated with Internet use. Some cable providers offer free local calls for some or all of the day, which makes them ideal for Internet access, although a handful prohibit this because it places a strain on their services. If in doubt, check with your cable company. If the service is available it can save you a fortune in phone bills.

COMPUTERS, YOUR HEALTH AND THE ENVIRONMENT

Computers can damage your health. Bad working practices (sitting in a fixed position at the keyboard for long periods, making awkward or repetitive movements with your arms, head or body) can contribute to a variety of ailments ranging from eyestrain to pain and discomfort in the limbs. Fortunately these are easily preventable. Taking time to ensure that your desk, chair and screen are positioned correctly can save days, even months of frustration and fatigue.

Health issues

Repetitive strain injury

Repetitive strain injury or RSI is a blanket term used to cover a collection of strain- and sprain-related health problems. Although there is some disagreement in the medical profession about whether or not RSI really exists, and if so exactly what causes it, a number of RSI sufferers are in no doubt that it is a work-related health issue. In extreme cases it can cause significant loss of flexibility in the hand and fingers.

If caught early and treated the effects can sometimes be reversed. But there is no guarantee that this will be possible; the damage produced by some kinds of RSI may lead to a permanent incapacity.

From the point of view of working at a screen RSI seems to be related to tendonitis and carpal tunnel syndrome (CTS), a disabling injury which can affect anyone who uses their fingers or wrists for long periods. Concert pianists and professional keyboard players have been known to suffer from CTS, which can sometimes be treated by surgery, though not always with success. It is much wiser to avoid the problem in the first place.

Keyboard

One of the biggest problems facing anyone who uses a keyboard every day is the way that the standard QWERTY keyboard is arranged. Conventional touch-typing can place severe strain on the wrist and finger joints. The hands can be cramped and often unsupported for long periods, the fingertips can be in almost constant use, and the finger joints may be held in a strained position as well as being continually flexed.

One simple but effective solution is a wrist support. This is a simple foam pad placed in front of the keyboard on which the wrists can be rested comfortably while typing. A wrist support is highly recommended for anyone who works with a computer keyboard on a regular basis.

A more adventurous solution is to use another keyboard layout. The Dvorak keyboard – named after its inventor, John Dvorak – uses a different and more logical letter arrangement. Not only is it faster to work with, it is also easier to learn and produces less strain when used over long periods. Most keyboards come with keytops that can be detached with nothing more complicated than a small screwdriver, so the keyboard can be rearranged into the Dvorak layout. Some software, such as Windows for the PC, includes support for the Dvorak system as well as the QWERTY layout.

Another alternative is ergonomic keyboards. These are designed to fit the hands better and provide built-in wrist support, although they still use the standard QWERTY layout. Both Microsoft and Apple make models; the Apple design is split in the middle and can be swivelled to suit your ideal hand layout.

Opinions about these keyboards are mixed. Some users find they make a huge difference, others find they do nothing at all. Try out a keyboard at your local computer store and see for yourself before you decide whether or not to pay the extra.

VDU emissions

A computer screen is also known as a VDU or visual display unit and, like a television, emits radiation, although levels likely to be generated are well below those set out for limiting risk to health. A simple but expensive way to avoid the problem is to buy a good portable computer. These have screens which do not produce the same kind of hard radiation. Unfortunately these screens are still very expensive. The next best option is to choose a monitor that has been fully certified to the MPR II standard. This ensures that any stray radiation is below background levels.

A glare filter – a plastic, glass or mesh panel that fits over the front of the VDU – will not affect 'hard' radiation such as X-rays, as these need proper shielding, but advanced models can help with electromagnetic radiation. This tends to collect as charge on the screen – hence the 'crackling fingers' effect – and can, in extreme cases, have an effect on the operator's face and skin. If this is a problem, you may consider investing in an air ioniser. This adds a complementary charge to dust particles that balances out the positive charge from the screen. Glare filters can also be helpful in improving display quality and contrast, and hence in lessening eyestrain. Generally speaking, correct position will do more for glare than a bolt-on filter. Before buying a monitor look very thoroughly at it, with a glare filter fitted if you feel you need one. A good – or a bad – monitor can make a huge difference to the amount of stress you feel when using your computer.

Printers

Early laser printers produced ozone, a gas which can be harmful in high quantities. Some newer models use a slightly modified printing system which is ozone-free. Always make sure that the printer you are using is in a well-ventilated area.

Another health hazard is toner spillage. The toner for most printers is a very fine powder and can be messy if spilled. Spills – which are unlikely unless the toner case is broken – should always be cleaned up immediately, wearing protective gloves.

The problem with dot-matrix and daisy-wheel printers is one of noise. Many computer accessory stores sell acoustic hoods, which you place over the printer to deaden the sound. These are strongly recommended for daisy-wheel printers in particular and worth considering for dot-matrix designs.

The print head on a dot-matrix model can become very warm. When changing a ribbon avoid touching the print head until it has cooled down.

Bubble-jet printers are relatively safe. Apart from the very minor problem of ink spillage if you try to refill an ink cartridge, bubble-jet and ink-jet printers have no notably unhealthy side-effects.

Noise

Your computer should run quietly. The cooling fan should not be distractingly loud. Although this may seem like a minor point, unwanted noise can aggravate stress levels. If you plan to spend a long time in front of your machine make sure that it is quiet enough to enable you to work with some tranquillity. Also, arrange your work to ensure you leave the screen for frequent short breaks *before* the onset of tiredness.

Posture

To prevent long-term problems you will need to maintain a good posture and relax regularly while working. A good scheme to follow is a one-minute break every ten minutes, a ten-minute break every hour and a forty-minute break (at least) every three hours. Stress-management consultants and some alternative health practitioners are good sources of advice on how to rela while still working effectively.

EC directives

The EC has introduced a set of directives designed to prevent operator discomfort while working with DSE (display screen equipment). These came into force on 1 January 1993 and will become mandatory on 1 January 1997. If you are an employer you are required to follow these. In outline this means you must:

- provide a monitor which has clearly formed and well-defined lettering, no reflective glare and negligible radiation
- provide a footrest for anyone who asks for one
- provide a document holder which can be positioned so as not to require unnecessary movements
- provide a wrist support that enables the operator to adopt the correct posture.

These regulations are available from HMSO and though, in part, quite vague, they will go some way to ensure that as an employer you are aware of health issues and have a responsibility to act on them.

HEALTH CHECKLIST

Monitors
Clean! (And easily cleaned)
Low radiation, MPRII-rated
Adequate letter size and display contrast
Comfortable flicker rate
Comfortable on-screen colour scheme
Tilted and swivelled to a comfortable viewing position
At the right height
Fitted with a glare filter if necessary
Located out of direct sunlight, with brightness and contrast set comfortably

System units
No buzzes, squeaks, squeals or hums
Accessible without user having to strain

Chairs
Stable, moves easily
Good back support, including the lower back
Fully adjustable

Document holders
Easily adjustable

Lighting
No glare or direct lighting from any source shining into user's eyes

---

Electrical
All power connections made safe
Unavoidable trailing wires placed under flat rubber floor conduits

Desks
Worktop at a comfortable height
Matt, non-reflective surface
Sufficient free space (at least 6 sq. ft.) around the computer for papers, etc.
Located out of direct sunlight
Supplied with a comfortable footrest if necessary
No unnecessary obstructions underfoot (such as papers, wastepaper bin)

Keyboards
Fitted with a wrist support
Easily movable
Weighted to prevent sliding
Optional Dvorak layout
Optional ergonomic design

Printers
Acoustic hoods where necessary
Located in a well-ventilated area
Toner spills are cleared up *immediately*

Air ionisers
To remove positive ions from the immediate environment if necessary

Working practices
Regular breaks of at least ten minutes an hour, spent walking around rather than stretching at the desk
Regular relaxation periods, based on professional relaxation techniques.

For further information contact the Health and Safety Executive (see Addresses)

How 'green' are computers?

You may see computers advertised as 'green', and in this context the word means something very specific. 'Green' features imply a range of power-saving options. The computer only draws maximum power while you actually use it. After a period of inactivity it starts to shut down – the monitor, the main processor chip and perhaps the hard disk go into a low power 'standby' mode. This saves electricity and – in theory – has less of an effect on the environment.

To get a computer with power-saving features, you should watch out for the 'Energy Star' rating. This was introduced by the US government in an attempt to save energy on a national basis, but is now available in the UK as well. A computer with a full set of Energy Star features will use less electricity than one without. But the differences are likely to be minor.

LEGAL ASPECTS OF COMPUTER USE

The Data Protection Act

If you maintain any kind of information about living people on your computer, you may be liable to register with the Data Protection Registrar. This is a relatively painless process which costs a standard fee of £75 for three years. The penalties for not registering are much stiffer – up to £5,000 plus costs in a Magistrates Court, or an unlimited sum in the Higher Courts.

There are a small number of exemptions. If you use your computer for writing letters and the information you keep is used solely for that purpose, then you will not need to register. But if you start to include personal details – and these can include a name and basic contact details – you become liable for registration. Even if you do not need to register, according to the Act you should ask the people whose information you hold if they have any objections.

The other main exemption is the information used for payroll calculations. If you keep this and use it for no more than this then you are exempt. However, if you start to maintain credit histories and other details, such as payments to the Child Support Agency, then you will need to register.

You should register even if the information is kept on a computer that you do not own. If you contract out the maintenance of a list of details to a computer bureau, then you are still the person 'in control' of the records and should register accordingly.

Once you are registered, you must follow the code of good information-handling practice set down in the Act in the eight Data Protection 'Principles'. Broadly these state that personal data must be:

(1) obtained and processed fairly and lawfully
(2) held only for the lawful purposes described in the data user's register entry
(3) used only for those purposes, and disclosed only to those people, described in the register entry
(4) adequate, relevant and not excessive in relation to the purpose for which they are held
(5) accurate and where necessary, kept up-to-date
(6) held no longer than is necessary for the registered purpose
(7) accessible to the individual concerned who, where appropriate, has the right to have information about themselves corrected or erased
(8) surrounded by proper security.

If you are registered you will have to convince the Registrar that you are not collecting information unnecessarily. This can sometimes have surprising implications. In one case the Registrar was called in to deal with a video hire shop that was collecting the passport and driving licence numbers of its customers as a security measure. The Registrar advised the shop to stop this practice, as collecting this information was inappropriate in the circumstances. Registration will require you to look at the records you keep and to ensure you have good reasons why you need to continue keeping them.

For a free information pack about the Data Protection Act and details of how to register contact The Data Protection Registrar (see Address section at back of book).

Software piracy

Software piracy ranges from the organised black-market copying of software and manuals, to the use of illegal copies of a word-processing package in an office because 'no one need ever know', to the installation of a single copy of software at home obtained from a friend who bought it legally.

If you use pirated software – and some estimates suggest that almost half of all the software in use in the UK today is pirated – you are liable for prosecution. Although the police tend to concentrate on organised pirating operations, if you use a disk supplied by a friend, in theory you are still committing a theft and are liable for any proceedings.

Software is usually sold on a licence rather than an outright purchase basis. This usually means that your rights are limited to:

• using the software on one machine at a time
• making backup safety copies

You are not allowed to:

• use the software on two different machines at once (e.g., desktop and laptop)
• pass copies to a friend
• sell the software on, even second-hand.

Any of these actions could leave you liable to prosecution. Passing copies to a friend is particularly dangerous. All software includes a unique serial number. If copies with your number turn up in an investigation then you will be held responsible.

In general then, it is unwise to pirate or to use pirated software. This applies especially in an office situation where the software is spread across a network, or is installed on a number of PCs. This kind of semi-organised piracy is being vigorously pursued by the industry, and agencies such as FAST (Federation Against Software Theft) even run a hotline service where the public can provide tip-offs about piracy (see Addresses). In short, the best advice is – don't.

FURTHER READING

ALTHOUGH MOST computer magazines cover the same territory, there is a huge difference in readability, usefulness and value. At one end of the market are the unashamedly technical magazines aimed at readers who already have a good grasp of the subject and need the latest information to keep up with the rest of the industry. At the other end are the magazines which specifically cater for the uninitiated. In between are the new family-oriented lifestyle magazines. A recent development is titles specialising in the Internet.

Many magazines include software in the form of one or more floppy disks or a CD-ROM on the cover. These can be an invaluable source of product demonstrations and free software. Often magazines publish separate CD-ROM and floppy-disk versions of the same issue. The former cost maybe an extra £1, but include slightly more text and much more software.

You will also find free booklets which give further information on some aspects of computing. These can be an excellent source of information for beginners and a very good way to equip yourself with a 'free' set of tutorials and a reference library. What follows is a brief survey of the magazines available in June 1996.

Monthly professional PC titles

These are usually heavy on advertising and make few concessions to the absolute beginner. Many articles will be all but incomprehensible to anyone without a good grasp of the subject, although there will sometimes be a couple of pages – but no more – devoted to absolute beginners. A handful of titles try much harder to present information in a way that does not exclude readers without a technical background.

Personal Computer World (VNU Publications)
This is one of longest-running computer titles on the market. Apart from the usual blend of industry news and product reviews there are also company profiles and interviews, as well as occasional more general computer or information technology-based features.

Computer Buyer (Dennis Publishing)
A good general-purpose title, although sometimes perhaps too technically advanced for complete beginners. The main emphasis is on hardware and software news, comparisons and reviews. The comprehensive Buyer's Guide is unusually good.

Computer Shopper (Dennis Publishing)
There are useful sections devoted to computers other than the PC and Mac but much of the content is highly technical. A regular beginners' feature ('Ivan Iwannado') does its best to demystify a different part of computing each month, but is perhaps still a little technical for absolute beginners. The large question-and-answer section is a good source of technical hints and solutions. *Computer Shopper* has a very low cover price.

PC Plus (Future Publishing)
This magazine has the usual opinion, news, reviews and educational sections. Like the others, it is best suited to readers who have a grasp of the basics rather than absolute beginners. It has recently started to include regular free booklets, which can be extremely useful, and there is an informative, if not quite comprehensive, buyer's guide which lists most of the widely available software and hardware products in any month.

Byte (McGraw-Hill)
This is an American technical monthly written by and for computer professionals. Although good for anyone who wants to keep on top of industry trends, the content is far too challenging

for a beginner. There is an 'international' section, but most of the advertising does not apply to the UK.

Windows Magazine International (CPS Publications)
Another US title which, in spite of the name, is very much a typical PC monthly. Like *Byte* the advertising is mainly US-based, making it less than useful for UK readers. Better suited to the intermediate reader who already has a good grasp of PC basics.

What Personal Computer (EMAP Business Communications)
What Personal Computer has much less advertising than the larger titles. The content concentrates on 'how to' and introductory features and comparative reviews aimed primarily at the small business user. Reviews include usability ratings from ordinary computer users. A very useful 'faxback' service is available which supplies copies of older features from back issues, and a shortlist section lists recent reviews and ratings. *What Personal Computer* is an excellent source of hard information for anyone who wants to concentrate on using a computer without first learning how it works.

What PC? (VNU Publications)
This is a very basic and straightforward monthly which is unusually good for beginners. Each month a new topic, such as printers or portable computers, is covered in some detail. While not as thorough as some of the more professionally-oriented monthly magazines, it is a good place for complete novices to find explanations of jargon and other useful information.

PC Direct (Ziff Davis UK)
This magazine is aimed particularly at mail order buyers of PC equipment. Otherwise it is very much a typical PC enthusiast's monthly title.

PC Today (IDG Media)
Aimed explicitly at the small business user, this title is an excellent source of advice and information. Unlike the technical monthlies, it concentrates specifically on news and features of

interest to business users, as well as offering more general business-related tips and ideas.

PC Magazine (Ziff Davis UK)
PC Magazine specialises in in-depth comparative reviews. Hardware reviews are presented in simple bar-graph form and software reviews include usability and productivity studies.

PC Pro (Dennis Publications)
This title is aimed at the computer-literate professional user. It includes a comprehensive buyer's guide and list of industry contact numbers and addresses.

Practical PC (Practical PC Magazine, Ltd)
With the emphasis on 'practical', this is a good choice for anyone who feels intimidated by the bulkier titles. Information is pitched at newer, inexperienced users. A number of step-by-step tutorial format 'how-to' articles are included each month.

Fortnightly

PC Mart (Maze Media)
A fortnightly paper containing classified ads. Good source of bargains and computer book reviews but not much solid buying advice.

Monthly PC leisure titles

Leisure titles concentrate on games and entertainment. They are written in a much friendlier and chattier style than the professional titles, and this can make them much less intimidating to beginners. They are also likely to include reviews of non-business multimedia software such as animated story books for children, encyclopedias, and other general knowledge and specialist-interest software products.

A relatively recent development is a range of leisure titles aimed at home and family users. These cover a wide range of computer-related subjects and include many articles pitched at beginners.

Some leisure titles concentrate specifically on games. They have been excluded from the list that follows.

PC Advisor (IDG Media)
Aimed specifically at beginners and family users, it is very reasonably priced and also reasonably comprehensive. However, the presentation is perhaps not as clear and focussed as it could be.

PC Format (Future Publishing)
This title concentrates on games and is aimed largely at younger readers, but also includes general-interest articles, interviews with writers, artists and musicians as well as computer professionals, and reviews of leisure software.

PC Home (IDG Media)
Similar in style and content to *PC Format*, but without the general-interest articles and articles, *PC Home* concentrates on games and multimedia titles.

PC Review (EMAP Images)
Although *PC Review* resembles other leisure titles it has a wider coverage and includes more news and general semi-technical features. Most of the pages are devoted to games-related subjects, but there are also useful reviews of other general-interest titles and hardware.

PC Answers (Future Publishing)
This is a general leisure title.

Computer Life (Ziff Davis UK)
Aimed squarely at the home and family user, *Computer Life* offers a wide mix of computer-related topics including games, education and entertainment software reviews, general-interest topics, the Internet and news. A 'family PC' section concentrates on software for younger users.

PC Guide (Future Publishing)
Originally a family-oriented monthly, this has now changed course and become a more general interest PC magazine, with

simple 'how to' features for beginners and information and stories about colourful and creative computer applications that affect everyday life, such as computer-generated special effects in films.

Monthly Apple titles

Apple titles tend to carry far less advertising than PC titles. Some PC monthlies are more like phone directories, which can make them unwieldy to read and store. Apple-specific monthlies are much more typical of other magazines.

As befits their readership profile, Apple magazines tend to concentrate on creative and artistic applications. But there is usually plenty for the home and business user too.

The Mac (Dennis Publishing)
This title contains general reviews and computer-related lifestyle features but little hard information for beginners. The most useful section is the comprehensive list of Apple software at the back.

MacWorld (IDG Communications)
A good choice for the professional Apple user, *MacWorld* tends to cover the traditional Apple areas of image processing, desktop publishing and creative design.

MacFormat (Future Publishing)
Mac Format covers the full range of Mac software from business to games and creative applications. There is a wide range of reviews, hints and tips and the content is suitable for beginners.

Fortnightly Apple titles

MacUser (Dennis Publishing)
An up-market version of *The Mac*, *MacUser* is one of the more informative Apple titles. It covers a wide range of software, not just the usual graphical and artistic applications, and there is even a 'getting started' section for beginners, although this tends to be aimed at Apple users with some basic experience rather than complete novices.

Weekly titles

MicroMart (MicroMart UK Ltd)
Cheap, printed on cheap paper, it includes some of the best computer bargains around. This is one of the best available sources for cut-price hardware and software bargains. Also has pages of free classified ads.

Internet publications

Internet (EMAP publications)
Internet includes features aimed at both beginners and more experienced users, although the style is always approachable and non-technical. The title is distinguished by its comprehensive directory section which includes an Internet glossary, full details of UK service providers and a huge selection of Internet locations and services.

Internet Advisor (VNU Publications)
This is a fairly dry Internet monthly aimed at the business user. A basic understanding of the Internet is assumed, and the magazine concentrates on long term planning and business strategies which are Internet-related. A good source of hard information about possible future developments and their practical applications.

Internet Today (Paragon Publishing)
Covers a broad range of Internet-related topics and takes a more accessible and less glamorous approach to its subject matter. It includes coverage of bulletin boards as well as the Internet, and is the only magazine to feature a regular BBS directory. Articles are aimed at beginners rather than experts, and also include general-interest features.

.net (Future Publishing)
This title includes 'how-to' introductory features. There are useful lists of places to look for software and a directory of Internet Service Providers in the UK.

NetUser (Paragon Publishing)
NetUser focuses on Internet service providers and Internet locations. Unlike the other titles this one is quarterly.

Wired (Wired Ventures Ltd)
Wired is more of a lifestyle and general-interest than a technological monthly, and more than any other it captures the flavour of interactions on the Internet.

Books

It can be worth taking your time to browse when buying computer books, because they can save you money in the long run. Many titles are expensive – expect to pay anywhere from £15 to £50 – but this should be taken in the context of other computer-related training materials. A one-day training course can cost you £150, and will not necessarily tell you any more than a book will (although you will be able to ask questions). So good books are a wise investment, and you may find that if you work through a well-written off-the-shelf tutorial you will not need to take a training course at all.

A trip to any bookshop will show that there is an almost unlimited number of titles available. It is impossible to recommend specific titles as your choice will depend on your own needs and learning style. For example, many computer books for novices take a humorous approach, and some readers respond well to this. Others simply find it annoying. The depth of the information presented and the overall layout vary tremendously too.

When starting from scratch you should budget around £100 for books to get you started. This will give you a good range to choose from, and you should be able to find everything you need to master the basics of the subject.

As a rough buying guide points to watch for include:

Style The most effective titles are those that take a step-by-step tutorial approach. Some books take a different tack and are meant as reference works. They may well contain everything you need to know but it will not be presented in a simple, easy-to-follow way. Unless you are already proficient in the applications covered, reference-style books are best avoided.

Accessibility If you can get to the end of the first chapter without understanding a word – and this is possible, even with some of the titles aimed at beginners – consider another title instead. Some authors fall into the trap of using jargon without explaining it first. This can be annoying and confusing, and does nothing to help you master the subject. A good book will make the subject seem easier rather than harder.

Relevance New versions of software are being released all the time, so you will need to check that a book on a specific software title applies to the version you have.

Many computer books are written and printed in the United States, and therefore use American expressions. Apart from the culture clash, this can sometimes render information inaccurate. Many Internet books, for example, include lists of Internet service providers. You should definitely look for an English title here, as American lists will not apply. In general, though, most US titles are suitable for the UK market.

Free software Some titles include free software. Check for a description in the book to see whether this will be genuinely useful to you.

ADDRESSES

Business software manufacturers and distributors

Although most of these manufacturers can be contacted via e-mail, this is usually reserved for contacting specific employees rather than for general public enquiries. Telephone in the first instance, or leave a message on one of the relevant support forums on CompuServe.

Connect Software
3 Flanchford Road
London W12 9ND
0181-743 9792

Intuit Ltd
3 Manor Court
Harmondsworth
Middlesex UB7 0AQ
(0800) 585058
On Compuserve:
GO INTUIT for general support

Lotus UK
Lotus Park
The Causeway
Staines
Middlesex TW18 3AG
(01784) 455445
(0990) 203000 (brochure line)
On CompuServe:
GO LOTUSWP for word-processor support
GO LOTUSA for spreadsheet support

Megatech Software
111-113 Wandsworth High Street
London SW18 4HY
0181-874 6511

Microsoft UK
Microsoft Place
Winnersh
Wokingham RG41 5TP
(0345) 002000
On CompuServe:
GO MSIC for general sales and other information

Novell UK
Novell House
London Road
Bracknell
Berkshire RG12 2UY
(01344) 724000
On CompuServe:
GO NGENERAL for general enquiries
GO NOVBG for buyer's information

Pegasus Software
Orion House
Orion Way
Kettering
Northamptonshire NN15 6PE
(01536) 495200

Quantam
Cowley Bridge Road
Exeter EX4 5HQ
(01392) 429424

Health

Health and Safety Executive
Books
Broad Lane
Sheffield S3 7HQ
(0541) 545500
For free copies of leaflets IND(G)
36 *Working with VDUs* and
IND(G) 153 *Computer Control*,
telephone (01787) 881165

Insurance brokers

Burnett & Associates
39-41 Victoria Road
Woolston
Southampton S019 9DY
(01703) 442227

First Domestic
Swan Court
Mansel Road
Wimbledon
London SW19 4AA
(0990) 500500
*(First Domestic offer a combined
insurance and support service)*

National Vulcan
St Mary's Parsonage
Manchester
M60 9AP
0161-834 8124

Tolson Messenger
148 King Street
London W6 0QU
0181-741 8361

Internet service providers

CompuServe UK
1 Redcliffe Street
Bristol BS1 6NP
(0800) 289378
E-mail:
70006.101@compuserve.com

Demon Internet
Gateway House
322 Regents Park Road
Finchley
London N3 2QQ
(0181) 371 1234
E-mail: sales@demon.net

Almac BBS
141 Bo'ness Rd
Grangemouth FK3 9BS
(01324) 666336
E-mail: info@almac.co.uk

Preprinted computer stationery

Paper Direct
Freepost (LE6296)
Hinckley LE10 0BR
(0800) 616244

Viking Direct
Bursom Industrial Park
Tollwell Road
Leicester LE4 1BR
(0800) 424444

Shareware libraries

The Public Domain and
Shareware Library (PC)
Winscombe House
Beacon Road
Crowborough
East Sussex TN6 1UL
(01892) 663298

Atlantic Coast Plc
The Software Source (PC)
The Shareware Village
Colyton
Devon EX13 6HA
(01297) 552222

MacPow (Mac)
96 John Street
Brierley Hill
West Midlands DY5 1HF
(01384) 481728

Stormont (Mac)
511 Upper Newtonards Road
Belfast BT4 3LL
(01232) 650537

Support providers organisation

The Computing Services &
Software Association
Hanover House
73–74 High Holborn
London WC1V 6LE
0171–405 2171
E-mail: CSSA@CSSA.co.uk

UPS and surge protector components

Farnell Electronic
Components Ltd
Canal Road
Leeds LS12 2TU
Sales: 0113–263 6311
Accounts: 0113–279 4444
Product support: 0113–279 9123

User groups

MacWorks Club (Apple
machines)
PO Box 2986
London NW11 8EA
0181–455 4750

The PC User Group (IBM-
compatibles)
84–88 Pinner Road
PO Box 360
Harrow HA1 4LQ
0181–863 1191
E-mail: info@pcug.co.uk

Voice dictation systems

Dragon Systems UK Ltd
Millbank
Stoke Road
Bishops Cleeve
Cheltenham
Gloucestershire GL52 4RW
(01242) 678581
(01242) 678575 (sales and
marketing)
E-mail: alanb@dragon.co.uk

Others

Data Protection Registrar
Wycliffe House
Water Lane
Wilmslow
Cheshire SK9 5AF
(01625) 545745
Fax (01625) 524510

Federation Against Software Theft
(FAST)
1 Kingfisher Court
Farnham Road
Slough
Berkshire SL2 1JF
(01753) 527999

INDEX